ABUNDANCE 101

Tools to
Activate and
Manifest a
Life beyond
your wildest
dreams

By Jason Snaddon

The Abundance Activator

First published by Busybird Publishing 2020

Copyright © 2020 Jason Snaddon

ISBN
Print: 978-1-925949-72-8
Ebook: 978-1-925949-73-5

Jason Snaddon has asserted his right under the Copyright, Designs and Patents Act 1988 to be identified as the author of this work. The information in this book is based on the author's experiences and opinions. The publisher specifically disclaims responsibility for any adverse consequences, which may result from use of the information contained herein. Permission to use information has been sought by the author. Any breaches will be rectified in further editions of the book.

All rights reserved. No part of this publication may be reproduced, stored in or introduced into a retrieval system, or transmitted in any form, or by any means (electronic, mechanical, photocopying, recording or otherwise) without the prior written permission of the author. Any person who does any unauthorised act in relation to this publication may be liable to criminal prosecution and civil claims for damages. Enquiries should be made through the publisher.

Cover image: Luke Stambouliah

Cover design: Busybird Publishing

Layout and typesetting: Busybird Publishing

Busybird Publishing
2/118 Para Road
Montmorency, Victoria
Australia 3094
www.busybird.com.au

Contents

Foreword	1
Introduction	5
Chapter One Your Focus Creates Your Reality	7
Chapter Two Reality Check	23
Chapter Three Land of Abundance	39
Chapter Four Intention & Vision	55
Chapter Five Taking Inspired Action	67
Chapter Six Harnessing the Universe to Support You	81
Chapter Seven Resistance & Attachment	91
Chapter Eight Purpose & Fulfillment	103
Chapter Nine Are We Really Spiritual Beings?	111
Testimonials	125
About the Author	127
Reference List	129
Notes	135

I dedicate this book to my sister, Gretchen. I hope my story helps you connect back to your angels, the ones I know you used to talk to when you were little.

Foreword

You are one very lucky person to be holding this book in your hands. If you apply the knowledge within its pages, it will make a huge difference in your life.

The guidelines within these pages will offer you a clear pathway to creating what you deeply and truly desire.

You will be entering into a journey deep into your inner world, asking: What is it you are truly, deeply seeking in life? Is it peace, prosperity a relationship or a more deeply attuned purposeful life?

Perhaps you are not happy about where you are heading and feel the need to transition to a new way of life … you will be heartened to know there are principles to follow and guidelines to assist you in really creating fulfilling and prosperous deeper life for yourself and those you love.

What does abundance mean to you? For many people it is elusive and frustrating, we may be flourishing in one area of our life only to be floundering in another.

My name is Julian Noel and I'm the founder of Shine Global, a global community of entrepreneurs and changemakers bettering the world through business. I work with people who are dedicated to creating a more abundant world for all of us and showcase them through live and online events.

Part of my role is to work with people to fill the gaps in their life and abundance is very often a blind spot. The knowledge in this book will shine a light into the dark corners where the lack of abundance lives.

I speak from having experienced working with Jason as a coach, and also from seeing the difference he has made to my friends, family and colleagues. Jason Snaddon truly is an Abundance Activator.

I met Jason in 2005 and marvelled as I watched his business, Love Property, grow. He was always at ease and in a state of flow around creating wealth. He worked with both intuition and data, his approach was sound, and he could back up his 'talk' with results.

I referred many people to him and was very happy to see him deliver results for all of them. He always told me his results were based on a set of principles and guidelines that anyone could follow.

As an event creator I had the responsibility of choosing and profiling the leaders and difference makers from all around the world. Finding qualified speakers on the topic of abundance was tricky: many of the people speaking about 'abundance' were often under resourced and were not living abundantly themselves.

Meeting Jason was a breath of fresh air, he lived abundantly, lived life on his terms, he had created a lifestyle that he had envisioned and was helping others to do the same. He walked his talk.

I see that purpose and prosperity are on the same continuum. For many people abundance is elusive, and this can cause great frustration and distress. It's best to make wise choices when we are faced with dilemmas. A friend gave me a piece of advice many years ago, 'Learn from masters, people who have already achieved what you are wanting to achieve.' Jason is a master.

Last year he contacted me to say he was stepping up to share and teach these universal abundance principles to others.

This is his first book and it's a cracker. Many people will benefit from reading it.

Enjoy.

Introduction

When I started out on this journey of abundance fifteen years ago, I had no idea that I would be coaching and teaching people this stuff. In fact, for many years I kept what I knew quiet except from those that I was on the journey with – I didn't even really share what I knew with my husband! I just got on with it, knowing that it worked.

I knew it worked because I set out in 2005 with a clear vision of what my Land of Abundance looked like and within five years it had all manifested. It continued to work as I grew Love Property, my real estate business, and my property investment portfolio. I knew if I was vibrationally aligned to whatever I wanted to create, it would manifest. My financial freedom also resulted as an added benefit.

When I lost my mum to cancer in 2014 it was the wake-up call I needed to finally share what I knew. Since then, I have coached and helped hundreds of people understand Abundance and align to what they truly want in their lives. I have opened up to the higher powers that are available to us as spiritual beings going through this human experience and I've also helped those I work with to access their own higher powers.

As you read these pages, you'll understand that abundance is not about just sitting, meditating and creating a vision. There is actually a process that you can follow that works. The more you face into how you show up, the greater the abundance you will ultimately experience.

It's my intention that as you take in the experiences and the teachings that I have to offer, you will be activated to create your own abundance.

Chapter One

Your Focus Creates Your Reality

My guess is you have picked up this book because you're looking for more abundance in your life. You wouldn't have picked it up if all areas of your life were amazing, right? You're probably also curious about why some people seem to 'have it all', while others continue to suffer.

Let me tell you, we are all worthy of leading abundant, joy-filled lives. We came to experience the wonderment of life. We came to experience joy, fulfillment, purpose and flow. The good news is that we are in the driver's seat of our own life and we all have the ability to make the most of it – to create life filled with abundance.

Have you ever noticed what you're thinking about? Most of us have stories running the whole time that we're not consciously aware of. Sadly, of the 60,000 thoughts a day that humans have, most of them are limiting thoughts, meaning that they're thoughts that hold us back, thoughts that are negative self-talk. I call it the 'chatter monkey mind' – our programmed subconscious thoughts that aren't particularly useful.

These unhelpful thoughts are what hold people back from living to their full potential. Interestingly, when we bring our awareness to what we're thinking about (at least some of the time) we can consciously change our thinking, and by changing our thinking we can change the outcomes.

The magic of focus

I first learnt about the concept of focus creating reality in 2004 when I was given William Whitecloud's book *The Magician's Way*. In this book, the first chapter is about the main character having a magic golf lesson. The lesson he learns is that when people are playing golf most of them are thinking about how to hold the golf club, how to stand and how to move the golf club. He calls this the 'swing circle' and recounts how golfers often get caught in their swing circle rather than just focusing on where they want the ball to go.

But when the focus is absolutely clear, a magician golfer allows his natural ability to get the ball to where he wants it; his natural ability enables him to hold and swing the club exactly as is necessary to make the shot. The character goes ahead and tries this. He gets out of his head – his thinking mind – stops trying so hard to get everything perfect and simply allows his natural ability and instincts to kick in. As he does that, the laws of the universe showed up to support him and the ball went where he wanted it to go.

What's wonderful is that this process is entirely replicable for us all, in any situation. I've had one of these 'magic golf lessons' where the teacher, Kris Barkway, helped me get that ball to exactly where I wanted it to go. It was a very tangible experience of magic.

In The Magician's Way, Whitecloud also talks about manifesting parking spots. I realised that I already practised this concept, without consciously understanding it. When driving alone I always find a parking spot effortlessly. I know now that this happens because I absolutely expect it to.

I remember when I was a boy my stepfather experienced the complete opposite. He always became frustrated and angry, driving around and around. I remember his words: 'I can't get a park, there are no parks here, it's too busy. Why are we out at this time?'

I remember thinking, this always happens like this. Now I realise why.

You see, your natural ability will spot a car space if you are aligned to thinking this. The universe, at the same time, helps support you to get what you want. When you are fully trusting and allowing, and completely unwavering in your knowledge that it will work, it will happen every time.

Beware though, it won't work if you have opposing forces in the car with you. So, if you, or anyone in the car, have thoughts that there won't be a park or it's going to be difficult to find one, sure enough you will have difficulty. Whenever I've had passengers in my car and realise that the parking manifesting isn't working, I drop everyone off and without fail I immediately find a spot. I proactively change the energy. Give it a try. Have fun with it – it's such a useful skill.

Curiosity provoked the process.

The focus concept in *The Magician's Way* is what got me started on my journey to abundance. I became more curious about trying out a new way of living, prompted in part by some challenges I was having in my career.

At the time, I was two years into being an investment property consultant and part of a team of fifteen consultants throughout Australia. I was driving all over the place seeing clients in their homes – mostly in the evenings – earning just enough to get by, but I wasn't certainly thriving.

In fact, I was considered one of the poorest performers. I was working long hours and working hard, and while I believed in what we were doing, I wasn't really enjoying it that much. In particular, I hated going away on the training courses, which happened each quarter. We would usually go to Queensland to see projects and for some reason I always felt uncomfortable and dreaded going. But I'll talk more about that later.

So, having read *The Magician's Way*, I started to use the ideas to improve my work life. I visualised having better meetings with my clients; I imagined my clients going ahead with the property solution I proposed, and my results started to improve. It felt like magic, but I knew that I had made it happen.

I thought, there has to be more to this. I felt a very strong pull to study these ideas further. I found out that William Whitecloud ran courses in Byron Bay and I knew that I needed to go. Unfortunately, I had missed the most recent one and the next one wasn't for a while, so I asked whether they had any courses in Sydney. It turned out he didn't, but his advanced students had just started teaching his work. Their business was called Dare to Be Remarkable and they happened to be running a course the following month. I immediately signed up.

To this day I remember clearly arriving at Walsh Bay in Sydney for the course. Walking ahead of me was a lady who, I thought to myself, was going where I was going. I knew that I was going to sit next to her. Sure enough, I followed her into the building and that was the beginning of my special and dear friendship with Fiona Findlay. We arrived at the most beautiful penthouse apartment overlooking Walsh Bay. I was then introduced to David Walker and Gisele Gambi, our teachers, who are now also my dear friends and colleagues.

I knew instinctively that I was meant to be at the course, and to this day it was one of the best decisions I've ever made in my life. As you will find out through the course of this book, the universe was very much at play in leading me there.

Throughout this book I will make reference to the universe. You may have another term for what I refer to as the universe, it could be God, higher self, source energy, oneness or all that is. Feel free to refer to this in whatever way you feel comfortable.

We are all intuitive beings

As we started on the course content, one of the first things I learnt was that we are all intuitive beings. We immediately got to try our intuition out; tuning in to what we picked up about each other, and my partner for the exercise was Fiona.

This intuition business made sense to me because I'd actually played with it before. When I'd had a few drinks, I loved to do readings on people (especially strangers), and they were always surprisingly accurate. So, I had fun with it – of course, sober this time!

What we learnt is that when we tune into our intuitive selves, we become powerful and expand. I discovered that by giving ourselves space to tap into our intuition about what we want, it comes through us from our higher selves or from a higher truth. In fact, we become unlimited by the rational mind.

It also became apparent that we can create from that place of intuition and that when we use our intuition, we open ourselves up to see what's possible from our unlimited selves and from our truth. By changing our focus to what we want and by using our intuition, we are infinitely more powerful and can create the life we desire.

For the first time I was truly creating space to see what I wanted in my life from my unlimited self. I realised that I could choose what I wanted, and that I could access this from an expanded perspective.

I also learnt that we are all limited by our thoughts and feelings. Humans have wounds, and most of the time these wounds drive our thoughts and feelings, especially the ones that are on repeat. But I learnt that we can change that story. When we shift our focus onto what we *do* want, we allow ourselves to override – and let go of – the wounding or limiting mind that can hold us back.

This was an amazing discovery for me.

Life audit

With this new knowledge in hand, for the first time ever I looked critically at all the different areas of my life to see where I was limiting myself and where I could change the story I had running through my mind. I broke my life up into the following categories:

- ⇒ Career & business
- ⇒ Finances
- ⇒ Relationships: love, family and friendships
- ⇒ Health & wellbeing
- ⇒ Home
- ⇒ Possessions
- ⇒ Travel & adventure

I assessed each area and what I found was that, other than my social life (which was very active), none of the other areas were in the shape I wanted them to be in.

I was quite recently out of a relationship and still adjusting to that. My career wasn't where I wanted it to be; I wanted to be the top sales consultant for the company I was working for, and I certainly wanted more money. The relationships in my family were not as strong as they could be. I was well, but I didn't really have a healthy lifestyle. I was renting with my ex-partner and had two investment properties that I was struggling to keep up with. I was driving an average car and living from pay cheque to pay cheque. I realised that I was just existing.

As part of the course, we were asked to do an evaluation of our lives and look at what had played out in relation to major events that we perceived as negative. We were asked to look for any recurring themes.

I spoke about the bullying I experienced at school from mostly older boys, and how I hadn't perceived myself as having a happy childhood. I also spoke about how I had always felt uncomfortable and unsafe around straight men in groups, and that this was playing out at work, particularly on the training trips. I discussed how I didn't share any of my personal life at work, even though I was out and happy as a gay man.

When I looked at everything, I could see that I was being small in my work environment, and that this was the result of a frequent theme from my childhood. What emerged was that I was playing 'insignificant'; I didn't see myself as being as good as the guys I was working with, and I didn't trust that I was safe to show my true authentic self. I realised that this was also contributing to how I related to my clients – I was always very private and reserved with them.

For the first time I could see how I was holding myself back. It was obvious that my focus had been on keeping myself safe, small and insignificant because I didn't trust the people around me enough to be my true self. This was such a massive realisation and seeing how that was holding me back in my career was a huge wake-up call.

I could finally see where my focus had been, and it certainly wasn't on what I wanted. It was only a perceived belief.

Did I want to continue this way, or did I want things to look different? I knew then that I had a choice. We are at choice all the time. That is the wonderful thing. We can play small and we can focus on what we don't want, or we can shift our focus onto what we do want, and at any time.

I could see that by playing small, by playing insignificant and not trusting those around me, that I had the results and outcomes to match these thoughts and expectations. I could see clearly that while the thoughts and feelings felt real, they actually weren't; they were simply my perception and my belief system.

When I saw how inauthentic I was being, I realised the limitations I had placed on myself at work. I also realised that I was in fact as good as the guys I was working with and that I could easily be the top consultant for the company if I chose to be. And I did choose to be! So, I shifted my focus to this decision and that was exactly what unfolded.

Within nine months of returning from Dare to Be Remarkable, I was the top consultant. I was completely different, in both my attitude and in my appearance. I stopped wearing a tie, I was real with my teammates, I was authentic with my clients and I was having more fun. New opportunities also presented themselves to me, as if by magic.

I had an inspired action come to me about placing an advertisement in the *Sydney Star Observer*, the LGBTQI community paper. From that ad I had a call from Michael Luca, a mortgage broker with Mortgage Choice. He invited me to be part of a networking group that he had created. I thought he might be able to refer me a few clients, but I had no idea just how fruitful this relationship would become. The wonderful thing was that I got paid more for the business that was referred to me directly, so, not only was I selling more properties, I was making more money too. That relationship continued to deepen and progressed to the point where I hosted the networking breakfasts.

This all evolved as a result of shifting my focus on to what I wanted and away from the limiting self; and from that space I'd created, the universe stepped in to support me way more than I ever could have imagined.

Gratitude keeps you on track

What's so interesting to me is that, regardless of having this knowledge and what I've seen in both my clients and myself, is that we forget to use it sometimes! Our limiting self seems to creep in quite often. I'm always looking for ways to remind myself of what works and to then create practises that keeps this negativity at bay.

One simple way I've found to help shift my focus and keep me on track to what I want is through gratitude. By being grateful we change the focus to what we do have rather than what we don't. The opposite of this is to focus on lack or the misery we are suffering. This can be seen in those people who are sick and who talk incessantly about being sick. Guess what happens? They keep getting sick. The more we practise gratitude and shift ourselves to remembering the good things we do have, the more it helps train our focus.

The fun thing is that we can also practise gratitude for things we might not necessarily have yet, but what we desire. For example, you might want to manifest a car. So, you'd say: 'I'm so grateful for the beautiful red Mercedes-AMG GT I have. I love seeing it parked in my garage.' You might have ill health, so you'd say: 'I'm so grateful for the amazing health and wellbeing I experience. I feel so vital and well.' The practise of gratitude proactively shifts the focus.

Here are some examples of gratitude phrases I use as regularly as possible:

⇒ I am so grateful for the abundance of money that flows in frequently.

⇒ I am so grateful for my beautiful home.

⇒ I am so grateful for the loving and fulfilling relationship I have with my partner.

⇒ I am so grateful that I earn over $300k a year from my coaching business.

⇒ I am so grateful for my portfolio of investments that continues to grow day by day.

⇒ I am so grateful for the endless clients that choose to work with me.

- I am so grateful for the delicious food I get to eat that nourishes my body.

- I am so grateful for the wonderful friends and family that I get to spend quality time with.

- I am so grateful for the support team that helps me grow my business.

- I am so grateful for the amazing travel I get to experience.

Try it out. The more you feel the appreciation the deeper you are in the frequency of that appreciation, and more of what you are grateful for will happen. Trust me, it works.

Affirm your focus

In addition to reciting phrases of gratitude, another way to keep your focus is to write out a list of affirmations and keep reading them or repeating them. You can also record them in the first person and play them back.

'I am ...' or, 'I have ...' or 'I choose ...' statements are very powerful.

Here are some to try:

- I have an amazing business that I love which is so abundant.

- I'm the top sales consultant for ...

- Money flows in easily and frequently; over $___ arrives into my bank account each year.

- I have a loving and fulfilling relationship with ...

- I'm happy and healthy.

- I live a full and fun life.

- ⇒ I'm powerful.
- ⇒ Wonderful opportunities keep coming my way.
- ⇒ I choose to live my best life.
- ⇒ I'm an amazing parent.
- ⇒ I'm an amazing wife, husband or partner.
- ⇒ I'm vital, well and energised.
- ⇒ I am amazing! I am amazing! I am amazing!

These statements, recited regularly, are very powerful especially when used in conjunction with a gratitude practice.

Be mindful that along the way it's easy to get off track; our old operating platforms and habits can come back into play. Whenever you're feeling dissatisfied, fearful, in reaction or you're not getting the outcomes you want, these are your cues to question yourself: Where is my focus? What am I thinking about? Am I thinking about what I don't want? The key is not to judge yourself for the answer... just accept it.

You could perhaps turn your thinking to more positive questions such as: What would I love? How do I really want to feel? What do I want my outcome to be? Practise gratitude for what is already in your life, revisit your affirmations, create a first person recording of all that you are choosing, and as you get used to it, tune in to your intuition. Ask yourself: What are my next steps? What is here for me? What am I inspired to do right now? You're not going to get it right every time. You will sometimes forget. The key is not to beat yourself up over it, but rather, realign and connect back into what you truly want.

For example, this very morning when I woke up, I felt anxious about writing, as I really wanted to complete this chapter today. I knew I needed to align myself to get it done, so I listened to a power meditation, which tapped me into my power and connected me into writing this book with ease and with the support of the universe. And it worked! As a result, this chapter has rolled out effortlessly.

Here is a link to that meditation: www.jasonsnaddon.com/meditations/

The universe supports your efforts

When you're fully aligned and unwavering in what you wish to bring forth, it will feel as though it happens easily – this is because the universe steps in to support you.

Let's discuss this concept further.

We're made up of energy. We are all vibrating as either an energy or as a frequency. All of our thoughts and feelings are a frequency. So, when our thoughts are in alignment, we emit that frequency and that then draws in other frequencies that are already in alignment. It's a case of what you put out, you receive back.

Gratitude is also a frequency. The more good feelings and thoughts you can create through gratitude for what already is, the higher your vibration is. It's from that vibration that you draw in more positive and empowered thoughts. That's how the Law of Attraction works. Your positive or negative thoughts bring positive or negative experiences into your life, just as energy attracts energy. And if we recognise that we are spiritual beings having a human experience, we know that we are capable of much more than what this physical human self allows.

When we can get ourselves into complete, unwavering, vibrational alignment with what we wish to manifest, the more we will be in the right frequency to easily draw it forth into our lives. For example, when I manifested becoming the top sales consultant for IPS, I made a conscious choice to be that and I was unwavering in the belief. I didn't know exactly how it would happen, but I knew that it would. I had to take inspired actions and one of them was to be my authentic self, the other was to place the advert in the Sydney Star Observer. Both of these actions, coupled with the resolute belief in my desire, all led to results far greater than I could ever have imagined.

The universe lined Michael up to see the advert, then we met, I joined the networking group, he referred clients to me, the networking group referred clients to me, and Michael's boss referred clients to me which eventually resulted in me working with other Mortgage Choice franchisees. I couldn't have planned all of that if I tried!

There is always an opportunity to harness these laws of the universe and to work with them. Remember that your focus creates your reality. So, have a clear intention and keep it on what you want and then ask the universe to support you.

Once you trust and know that it's underway, the more you are aware of the actions to take, which in turn leads to what you want manifesting itself.

Three things I'd like you to try:

1. Get a journal, pen and some water. Take some breaths and feel into your heart. Ask yourself: What would I love? What would I love to feel? What do I want to experience? Let your heart guide you.

2. Then ask yourself: What am I grateful for right now? Write down as many things as you can think of.

3. Listen to the power meditation.

    https://www.jasonsnaddon.com/meditations/

Chapter Two

Reality Check

To create or manifest what we want, we first need to be aware of our starting point. In order to move forward we must be honest with ourselves about where we are, and face into our current situation: 'Then you will know the truth, and the truth will set you free.' As quoted in the Bible.

Secondly, we must know that we can't have what we want without having the opposite experience. Otherwise, how else would we know what we already have isn't what we want?

Usually, we don't create change without a reason. Change typically takes place when dissatisfaction arises or when we become aware of wanting a solution to our current problem. Being really clear about what we want and then understanding where we are in relation to what we want is crucial.

So how do we do that? How can we be objective about our current circumstances? Most people don't regularly evaluate all areas of their life and give themselves a reality check. It can be hard to own up to the mediocrity or negativity. But this kind of 'life audit' is vital to understanding your current situation so you can then assess how far you are from what it is you desire. By creating space to see where each area of your life is you are creating a starting point for change, for expansion and for growth. You are allowing yourself to see what is working, what isn't working and what could be improved.

This may be confronting to begin with, but the more you allow yourself to go through this process, the more you will create reason and momentum to move forward with building the life you love.

It's my firm belief that we are spiritual beings that came from the universe to earth to have a human experience. However, in doing that, many of us forgot the truth of who we are, and in our humanness, we created suffering. I believe that we can go back and remember who we truly are, but to do this we must first experience who we are not.

A really powerful way to work through this process is to section off the different areas of your life and give yourself a rating out of ten for each – ten being amazing, you couldn't get any better, and zero meaning that it is non-existent or completely lacking in your experience.

So, let's list out the different areas of life worth doing a reality check on:

⇒ Career & business

⇒ Health & wellbeing

⇒ Relationships

    Romantic relationship

    Family relationships

    Friendships

⇒ Financial

⇒ Knowledge & learning

⇒ Social Life

⇒ Travel & adventures

- ⇒ Home
- ⇒ Spirituality
- ⇒ Giving Back

The final area you should rate is your overall sense of self and wellbeing.

Once you have an honest rating for each area you have a starting point for change. Begin with the area you ranked the lowest and ask yourself why this is. List out the reasons you've rated this area so low.

Let's take a look at how you might consider some of the main areas of your life.

Relationships

Let's use an example: you might have given your romantic relationship with your husband, wife or partner a low rating. Write down the reasons you rate this area as you do. Start with what you feel is lacking from your husband, wife or partner.

Some things could be:

- ⇒ We fight too much
- ⇒ The spark is gone
- ⇒ Our sex life is not what it was or could be
- ⇒ They drink too much
- ⇒ I feel like I am being controlled
- ⇒ They don't respect me
- ⇒ We don't have fun together

- ⇒ We don't spend quality time together
- ⇒ They work too much

Then flip it around. What are you, or aren't you, contributing to the relationship?

- ⇒ I lose my patience
- ⇒ I get angry with them
- ⇒ I don't feel close to them
- ⇒ I don't feel attractive to them
- ⇒ I also drink
- ⇒ I want to control them
- ⇒ I don't give them respect
- ⇒ I don't instigate fun or sex
- ⇒ I don't instigate quality time together

The more you can analyse how and if you respect your relationship, the more you can take responsibility. A relationship is a two-way street, there is always a mirror going on. Our partners, friends and family members will reflect back to us what we are putting out in some way.

So, the more you own up to where *you* are, the more you are able to create change. And the change comes from within first. This is really key to the process. We can't change others, but we can change ourselves. We can disagree with how others behave in our experience; however, we can love and accept them for where they are when we make positive changes to ourselves first.

Focus on yourself first – how am I behaving? How am I responding?

How am I expecting my partner to behave? Most of the time we are driving others to behave in a certain way because that's our expectation of them and so we basically set them up to fail or to let us down. This is typically unconscious behaviour, which makes it challenging to change if we're not aware of it.

When relationships aren't operating at their most abundant and there is struggle, there are victim, persecutor and rescuer dynamics playing out. Let's explore these.

Victims

Victims see themselves as helpless, oppressed, powerless, dejected and ashamed. They have a 'poor me' response. They can come across as sensitive and expecting special treatment from others. They can deny any responsibility for their negative circumstances and usually deny their ability to change those circumstances.

A person in a victim role will look for a rescuer or a saviour, and if someone refuses or fails to do that, they can quickly perceive them to be the persecutor.

Rescuers

Rescuers need to help others: 'Let me help you,' 'I'll do that for you.' Rescuers work hard at making sure everyone is okay and they need to help others to feel good about themselves. This usually comes at the detriment of their own needs and they often don't take responsibility for helping themselves.

Rescuers are usually co-dependent and are enablers. They need victims to help and often won't allow the victim to succeed or get better. They can use guilt to keep their victims dependent and feel guilty themselves if they aren't rescuing somebody.

Rescuers are frequently overworked and tired, with resentment building and festering. It's not a sustainable way of operating.

Persecutors

Persecutors blame others: 'It's all your fault.' Persecutors criticise the victim, set strict limits, and can be controlling, rigid, angry, authoritative and unpleasant. They keep the victim feeling oppressed through threats and bullying.

Persecutors aren't flexible and find it hard to be vulnerable. They fear the risk of being a victim themselves. Persecutors yell and criticise, but they don't actually solve problems or help others resolve a situation.

What I've outlined are the most extreme examples of these roles. In relationships we often take on these roles to some degree and play these games that hold our relationships in constant negative cycles. It's also common to move between the different roles depending on the situation or circumstance.

To keep the suffering at play, people will switch roles or cycle through all three without ever getting out of the drama. Victims need a saviour, rescuers need to save someone, and persecutors need a scapegoat.

Ask yourself, 'What roles do I predominantly play in my relationships?' The starting point to making change is seeing what is currently playing out. So, if you have any relationships that are out of balance, go back and reflect on this exercise with a particular person in mind.

Finances

How did you rate your finances? Most of us have blocks around money and money flow, usually because of the beliefs our parents have instilled in us. Unless we get clear on where our finances currently are, how can we change it?

Do the same as you did with the relationships and list out the reasons why you rated your finances as you did.

Maybe you're telling yourself:

- ⇒ I don't have enough money
- ⇒ I live week to week or pay cheque to pay cheque
- ⇒ There is just enough to get by, but not much more than that
- ⇒ I or we can't afford this or that
- ⇒ I just make ends meet
- ⇒ I'm in debt
- ⇒ There isn't enough money to do …
- ⇒ We fight about money …
- ⇒ I don't save or invest for our future
- ⇒ I or we haven't planned for retirement …
- ⇒ I can't stop working
- ⇒ I never have enough
- ⇒ There's not enough for everyone

Some of these will possibly be real, but some of them will only be perception.

It's time to get real with your financial position. Create a spreadsheet with four columns: asset, value, debt and equity. List out all of your assets with an approximate value; include your superannuation, shares, property and any savings or money you have in the bank. Then list out all your debts and liabilities.

See the example below:

ASSETS & LIABILITIES

Asset	Value	Debt	Equity		
6 Sunshine st, HappyLand (Principal Home)	$950,000	$609,000 ANZ Bank	$341,000		
45 Abundance Pl, Joyville (Investment Property)	$380,000	$186,000 AFG Bank	$194,000	$385	Per week
Property assets sub totals		$795,000	$535,000		
Joint Savings	$8,000		$8,000		
2018 Mazda 3	$26,000	$18,000	$8,000	$783 pm	
2015 Toyota Yaris	$14,000		$14,000		
Superannuation Balance	$80,000		$80,000		
Superannuation Balance	$68,000		$68,000		
Shares	$4,000		$4,000		
Credit Card Debt		Nil			
Sub Totals	$1,530,000	$813,000	$717,000		
NET WORTH $717,000					

Knowing your numbers is crucial. Most people don't have any idea what their financial position is. Remember, it's impossible to move forward without knowing where you are right now. I review my financial position three times a year – at the beginning of the calendar year, the end of the financial year and when I do my taxes.

Now that you know your numbers, whatever they are, you have a starting point to move forward. Are your numbers better than you thought or worse than you thought? Whatever your answer, don't judge yourself. The great thing is that now you know, and this is where you need to be in order to create a better position. You must have awareness and know the truth of your current situation.

The next step is to run a quick budget. There are plenty of amazing apps you can download on your phone to help with this. Goodbudget is great as it also brings awareness to conscious spending. A budget is purely for you to get clear on what's happening with your cash flow, so, again, don't judge yourself, just acknowledge and accept.

Now you have your financial starting point you can make plans to move forward into a more positive position.

Health and wellbeing

List out the reasons you rated your health and wellbeing as you did.

Maybe you're telling yourself:

- ⇒ I'm unfit
- ⇒ I feel overweight
- ⇒ I'm not doing enough exercise
- ⇒ I eat unhealthily
- ⇒ I don't get enough sleep
- ⇒ I don't have enough energy
- ⇒ I crave sweet things
- ⇒ I drink too much
- ⇒ I eat junk food

You might like to bring your awareness to what you're consuming each day. Are you conscious of what's going in your body or are you unconsciously consuming food and drink? Do you binge at particular times of day or in certain situations?

Now it's time to consider your movement. Do you take regular walks with the dog? Is your job sedentary? Are you going to the gym or participating in sports? Could you find a few more minutes each day to move your body?

Keep going until you feel complete.

Career or business

How did you rate this area of your life?

Consider these questions:

- Do you love what you do? If so, why? If not, why not?
- If you do love what you do, what areas are there for improvement?
- Are you clear on why you do what you do?
- What is the why?
- Do you see what you do as fulfilling?
- Do you feel energised with what you do or does it deplete you of energy?
- Does what you do align with your values?
- Are you being paid or paying yourself enough? If not, why not?
- Do you enjoy working with your colleagues/team?
- If you're employed, are you happy with the leadership?
- If you run a business, are you happy with how it looks?
- Where is it limited?
- Do you have a happy and engaged team in your business?
- Are you happy with customer engagement and service?
- Are you happy with your marketing and reach?
- Are you clear on your brand?
- Do you work on the business as well as in it?

- ⇒ How is your time management?
- ⇒ Are you paying yourself first?

Most of our waking hours are at work, regardless of whether we work for someone else or ourselves. So, if you're not enjoying what you do, that means you're spending most of your waking hours doing what you don't want to do. Is it worth your valuable time doing something that does not give you joy?

Remember, you ultimately get to choose how you spend your time.

Knowledge & learning

Are you expanding? Are you learning new things and trying out new experiences? Reading this book is one form of expansion, so well done for taking this step.

Ask yourself:

- ⇒ Am I closed off to new ideas?
- ⇒ Do I have an open mind or am I relying on what I already know?
- ⇒ Do I proactively seek new knowledge for my career or business, or do I only seek new knowledge for fun?
- ⇒ When was the last time I actively sought out a situation where I could learn something new and expand my horizons?

Travel & adventures

Ask yourself:

- ⇒ Am I giving myself space to travel, to see new things and to have adventures?

- ⇒ Do I even know what's out there?
- ⇒ When was the last time I got out of my comfort zone?
- ⇒ When did I last go somewhere on a whim?

Experiencing new cultures and environments is good for us. It expands our thinking, builds understanding and empathy and helps us contribute to the world in a positive way.

Home

Ask yourself:

- ⇒ Do I love where I live?
- ⇒ Is my house a home?
- ⇒ Do I feel comfortable, safe and happy in my home?
- ⇒ Do I love the city, the suburb or even the country I live in?
- ⇒ Is my home a sanctuary?
- ⇒ Do I enjoy inviting people to my home or am I embarrassed by it?
- ⇒ Do my friends and family feel comfortable in my home?

Answer these questions honestly. Remember, you don't have to stay put if you aren't truly comforted by your home. You always have a choice.

Spirituality

How did you rate this part of your life? Did you even give it a rating? It's an area that is often neglected. I know when I started my personal growth journey, I considered my spirituality non-existent. Spirituality doesn't necessarily mean organised religion – it's whatever it means for you. Spirituality is about being concerned with the human spirit or soul, rather than material or physical things. It's about having a sense of connection to something bigger than ourselves. Simply take time to consider how your spirituality is being nurtured – or not – and what it could mean for you if you positively changed this aspect of your life.

In the last chapter of this book I will be sharing more on the subject of us being spiritual beings having a human experience.

Giving back

Abundance is as much about giving back as it is receiving. Giving back isn't just giving gifts or donating money or time, it's also about how much you give of yourself; how much you give in service to others, your community or the environment. It's also about how well you think of others, your community or the environment as well as our actions.

When we choose actions that bring happiness and success to others, then we will experience success and happiness for ourselves. So, it's important to ask yourself what are the consequences of this choice I am making? Will this choice bring happiness to me and those affected by this choice?

Now that you've reviewed your current reality you might be feeling a little bit uncomfortable. This is a good thing and should be embraced. As I said, facing into where you are is so important as it represents the starting point from which you can grow. It's this truth that will set you free. Well done for going there.

By owning up to where you are, you're already moving forward into your vision. You can now begin to shift your focus on to what you want.

You are now ready to create your Land of Abundance.

Chapter Three

Land of Abundance

Now that you've assessed each area of your life – and admitted where you are and how you feel about it – it's time to decide how you would like everything to look. What would you love your life to be like in all aspects?

What is the Land of Abundance?

I first discovered this concept back in 2005. I was led on a meditation journey to my Land of Plenty – a utopia that provides for all of our desires and needs.

Essentially, I tapped into my intuition – my higher self – to see what was possible and what was available to me if I so chose it. It was a truly enlightening experience.

As time went on and I continued to connect with my Land of Plenty I realised that this was actually my Land of Abundance, a place that's all about giving and receiving.

Your Land of Abundance is a place where there aren't any limits, where you can truly allow your imagination to expand and where you can daydream about what you would love most in your life.

By connecting into your intuition – a space where the rational mind is out of the way – you can realise that there are no reasons why or why not, just pure potential and pure allowing.

At this stage you don't need to know how or when it's all going to unfold, it's about allowing yourself to see, sense, feel and experience what is possible.

My Land of Abundance

When I first tapped into what was possible back in 2005, I could see that I wanted to be the top sales consultant for the company that I worked for. I could see that it was possible for me to have my own business doing what I was doing. I also clarified with myself that I wanted a loving and fulfilling relationship with someone. I could see us living in a beautiful penthouse apartment with views. I could see that we were independent, that he had his own career but that we had shared values. I could see that it would be a deeply loving relationship. I could see a Mercedes convertible, a portfolio of properties, I could see strong friendships and closeness in my family, and I could also see myself giving back to the community.

In fact, community was a big theme that came up repeatedly. I could see plenty of travel and adventures. I could also sense feeling vital, fit and healthy. And of course, to have all of that meant I had an abundance of money; I could see that I created a means to generate a good income as well as investments. This, in a nutshell, was my first Land of Abundance.

So, it's all well and good to visualise a Land of Abundance, but what do you actually do with the vision? I broke it down into the different aspects I wanted to work on so that I could clarify what actions would be necessary.

I wanted to:

- ⇒ Be the top sales consultant
- ⇒ Have a great income and investments
- ⇒ Operate my own business

- ⇒ Be in a loving relationship
- ⇒ Have a new home
- ⇒ Improve my family relationships
- ⇒ Nurture valuable friendships and my social life
- ⇒ Improve my health and wellbeing
- ⇒ Go on great travel adventures
- ⇒ Give back to my community

Another aspect of our lives to consider, which interestingly didn't show up in my Land of Abundance in 2005, was 'spirituality'. Personal growth and the Law of Attraction were as far as my spirituality went at that point. But I did commit myself to keeping on this path of abundance by keeping my focus on what I wanted!

Land of Abundance practice

If you're now ready to create your own Land of Abundance you can either follow this link to the Land of Abundance meditation or work through the process below: https://www.jasonsnaddon.com/meditations/

1. Close your eyes, take a few deep breaths, let yourself feel relaxed, allow any thoughts or feelings to arise and then release them with each breath.

2. Imagine a beautiful place – perhaps it's a beach or a forest – in as much detail as you can. The air, the warmth, the sun, the breeze, the taste, the smell. Imagine as much of this beautiful place as you can.

3. As you imagine this place, know that this is your special place, it's your Land of Abundance.

4. Allow your imagination to tell you what you're doing, what you're wearing, how you feel, who is there with you and start imagining all the areas of your life at their most abundant and most expansive. Your finances, your relationships, your home, your health and wellbeing, your career or business, what you're doing for fulfillment, your friendships and social life, your community (are you giving back in some way?), your travel and adventures, your car, your home. Allow your imagination to keep expanding.

5. When you feel ready, gently open your eyes and put pen to paper to capture as much as you can. Keep going until you feel complete. For some of the areas you may get images, you may get words, or you may simply feel what is around you. It's all perfect. Capture as much of it as you can without judging or questioning. Simply let it all come out.

You may question whether the vision is a result of tapping into your intuition or into your mind. The answer is, it doesn't really matter at this stage. The more you have the intention to connect to your intuition the more it will come from your intuition. The mind always needs to decipher what our intuition is telling us anyway, but at this stage we're just in the creation mode, so we don't want to connect to any rational or limiting thoughts – as soon as that happens, it ceases to be intuition. If it helps, you can call it 'my imagination'. Allow your imagination to create your Land of Abundance; let it take you on the journey.

It's possible that you'll get stuck on what you want to create. This will most likely happen when the limiting mind takes over. The key here is to start with what you can see and what you can imagine. The more you explore this, the more you will receive.

Remember, this is for your own expansion, so make it as fun and joyful as you can.

Now that you have your Land of Abundance outlined, break it down into the different areas:

⇒ Career or business

⇒ Finances

⇒ Relationships – love, family, friends

⇒ Home, car, furnishings

⇒ Health & wellbeing

⇒ Travel & adventures

⇒ Giving

⇒ Community

⇒ Vision Board

The next step is to create a vision board of what you've created in your Land of Abundance practice. A vision board is a tangible symbol of your desires and aspirations and can serve as a great tool to motivate and inspire you towards action.

The more you can include on your vision board that represents your Land of Abundance and the more you have good feelings towards it, the more it will unfold. Placing your vision board where you can see it often throughout the day will help you create your Land of Abundance effectively, because you essentially do short visualisations each time you look at it. So, spend some quality time cutting out pictures from magazines or downloading images to represent your Land of Abundance.

Once you can clearly see each aspect of your Land of Abundance you can tap into them separately to start bringing them forth. You do this by simply choosing an area to focus on, then by setting a clear intention: 'I choose to have ...'

Here's the way I chose to allow my Land of Abundance to unfold:

- 'I am the top consultant for IPS.'
- 'I choose to draw forth over $200,000 income a year.'
- 'I choose a loving and fulfilling relationship with a beautiful man.'
- 'I choose to create an amazing and beautiful home that we own.'
- 'I choose loving and fulfilling relationships with my family.'
- 'I choose loving, fun and fulfilling relationships with my friends.'
- 'I am vital, well and energised.'
- 'I choose a vibrant and balanced social life.'
- 'I choose amazing travel and adventures.'
- 'I choose to give back to the community in a fun and fulfilling way.'

The important thing is for you to put these categories in your own language, but to keep it succinct and relatively broad so that you don't limit it. I have, however, always found it most affective to start the statements with 'I am' or 'I choose'. An 'I am' statement suggests it has already happened, which is a very powerful way to manifest your desires.

By focusing on each of the different areas, you create space to see what they look like at their most expanded. For example, let's say you choose to create a business. What would your product or service be? Where would it be located? What attributes does it have? How does it feel running this business? Imagine who your clients are. Do they love your products or services? Does this business give you a sense of purpose and fulfilment? Who is working in the business with you? Imagine the abundant revenue, the profits and the happy customers. What does the happiness create for you?

Imagine yourself going there each day, imagine it feeling like fun, the joy, the amazing team supporting you. The brand and the offerings. The clearer the picture and the more you feel good about that picture, the more you are shifting your frequency to align with it.

The more you can expand and then focus on each area, the better. So, daydream about them. Consciously choose to visualise these things as if they have already happened. Keep visiting your vision board.

Gratitude

Another powerful way to manifest your Land of Abundance is through gratitude. Not only gratitude for what you already have, but you can also be grateful for what you're drawing forth. For example:

> *'I'm so happy and grateful for my beautiful home. I'm so grateful for the abundance of money that flows in. I'm so grateful that I'm the top sales consultant. I'm so grateful for all the amazing clients that I work with. I'm so grateful for how healthy well and energised I am.'*

When you can say, feel, see, sense and experience gratitude, the more abundance you will feel, sense and experience.

Say it as though it's happened

Another powerful way to keep your focus on what you want is to record yourself describing your Land of Abundance. Say it in the first person, as if it's already happened. For example:

> 'I love the fabulous home that I live in with my beautiful partner, husband or wife. I'm so abundant that money flows in all the time. My business is successful and fun, and I have amazing clients. I have wonderful friendships, a rich vibrant social life and my relationships with my family are happy and fulfilling.'

You should then listen to the recording as often as possible. You need to create good feelings and thoughts around your Land of Abundance, so that you adjust to that frequency of drawing it forth.

At this point, your mind might start doubting and questioning with limiting thoughts or feelings. When you can notice them and let them be felt and heard, by doing so, you will move through them. But don't get stuck here. Once they've been felt and heard, revisit your vision board, your recording or whatever you need to do to get reconnected and back on track.

The other thing that might happen is that you may not feel any traction for a while. Again, it's about being okay with that and trusting and being unwavering in your knowledge that it's unfolding. You could even say to yourself, 'I'm so grateful that my Land of Abundance is unfolding day by day.'

In summary:

1. Create space, meditate and imagine your Land of Abundance. Be sure to cover all areas of your life.

2. Create a vision board that clearly represents your Land of Abundance.

3. Record a description of your Land of Abundance in the first person.

4. Practise gratitude.

The more you can detach, trust and allow, the better. Be unwavering in your thoughts that your Land of Abundance is unfolding in divine timing. Trust this. Know this.

Some of you might be thinking that this feels a bit selfish, because it seems as though it's all about material outcomes. At this stage it is. However, that's perfectly fine. It's okay to be selfish about going for what you want in a material sense. There is enough abundance, there is enough money and things for everyone to benefit from – no one needs to miss out.

It's important to note however, that from this place of 'selfishness' we move into selflessness – the wonderful next phase of abundance. Selflessness is when we're able to, or choose to, give back. And it looks different for everyone. For me, I experienced abundance by way of material possessions first and then I gave back to the community by volunteering to be on the board of the Sydney Gay & Lesbian Business Association. I was passionate about helping small business people have a safe space to network. I also wanted to support young people in need and was trained by the Salvation Army. These opportunities were fulfilling and valuable to me as much as they were to the community.

Don't concern yourself if you're not ready to go down the path of giving back just yet. The starting point is to be in true alignment with what you would love for yourself right now. Go for it with gusto.

In 2010, five years after allowing my Land of Abundance to be seen, it all unfolded.

Chapter Four

Intention & Vision

Now that you have a clear picture of your Land of Abundance, the next step on your journey is to break down each aspect and expand each vision through intention setting. By setting clear intentions for each area of your life, you allow yourself to create a deeper level of focus on what is really possible. The intentions help make the visions become a reality.

To do this you either choose what you are wishing to create or be that. Writing your intentions clearly in a dedicated journal, with 'I choose', 'I am' or 'what would it be like' statements is a powerful way to cement what you've decided to create.

Let's say you've visualised a beautiful home for your Land of Abundance. The next step to manifesting it is to say or write something like: 'I choose for my beautiful home to manifest', 'I choose to see my beautiful home', 'I am living in my beautiful dream home', 'I choose to manifest my dream home' or 'What would it be and feel like to live in my beautiful home?'

Perhaps you want to focus first on your health and wellbeing. You might say things like: 'I am vital, well and energised', 'I am fit and healthy', 'I choose to be vital and well' or 'What would it be and feel like to be vital, well and energised?'

Maybe you'll choose to work on manifesting a beautiful and loving relationship. You might say things like: 'I choose to allow a beautiful partner to enter my life', 'I choose a loving and fulfilling relationship with a beautiful person', 'I'm living in my dream relationship with my perfect partner' or, 'What would it be and feel like to be in this beautiful relationship?'

Likewise, you could have a vision of the other relationships in your life, such as: 'I choose to have loving and fulfilling relationships with my family', 'I choose to have fun and joyous friendships', 'I'm grateful for the beautiful relationships I have with my friends and family' or 'What would it be and feel like to have these loving and fulfilling relationships?'

You can also do this for manifesting money: 'I choose to earn over $ ...', 'I'm wealthy and successful', 'What does this feel like?' or 'I choose for money to flow to me effortlessly.'

You can create clear intentions for anything that you would like to manifest. To do so, bring awareness to your heart, allow your heart to open up to the intention and allow your heart to connect into every minute detail of whatever it is you desire. For example, your dream home. What does it look like inside and out? Where is it? What is it made of? How do you feel both inside and outside it? What are the gardens like? Describe it as clearly as you can imagine it. Feel how good it is to be there. Imagine who is there sharing the house with you, who comes visiting. What does your life look like living there? Engage all the senses: what can you smell? What can you taste? What can you hear? What is activated in you? Connect with as much as you can and then write out as much as you possibly can. Read it back – is there more you can add? How does it feel? Do you believe it? Are there any doubts, fears? Is there any disbelief?

The next step is to list out your present state in relation to this vision. Do you currently have the deposit, the income or the savings? Own up to your current reality. Are there any fears or doubts about allowing this house into your life? Do you believe that you are worthy of such a home? Do you feel any resistance in your body? If so, where? What is the feeling? What does it look like? If it had a colour what would it be? If it had a shape what would it be? If it had a texture what would that be? If it had a temperature what would that be? Now rate it for intensity out of ten, with ten being almost unbearable and zero being nothing. Just notice it. By facing into where you are, you own up to the truth of what is.

Now you've created tension. The reason for this is that you have aligned to what you want, and you've owned up to where you are at in relation to it. You have a clear starting point, a clear vision and hopefully excitement for your vision as well. There is the tension and that tension will want to resolve. But in order for it to resolve, you must take action.

So, how do you take inspired action in relation to manifesting your new home vision? First, bring your awareness to your heart, then bring your awareness to your home. Visualise your dream home with intense clarity, then ask your heart, 'Heart, how many inspired actions are there for me to take to move me forward at this time?' You will always get the number, and you will always receive what you are ready for. The important thing is to take the action no matter how small it may seem.

New relationship manifestation

To manifest a relationship, you need to list out all the attributes you would love in your relationship, as well as the physical attributes in your partner. This is a private list, so feel free to write anything.

For it to work, you must be ready to manifest this relationship. If you're coming from a place of lack, neediness or from attachment, it won't work. But if you're coming from a place of readiness and trust, and that you feel that you're ready to give and to receive from this relationship, then you're ready. Remember though, it's in the perfect (divine) timing for all parties so you must release all of your attachments to when it will manifest.

Ask yourself, 'Am I truly ready?'

I did this exercise in 2006 and I was ready. I sat quietly, felt my heart and I said to my heart, 'I am ready to manifest my relationship.' I listed out on a piece of paper all the attributes I was choosing. I kept listing everything I could think of until the page was full. I re-read it and said the following invocation:

> *'Dear universe, I am ready. I am ready for my beautiful partner to enter my life. I am ready for my beautiful love relationship to manifest. I am ready, I am ready, I am ready. Please send him in divine timing. Please guide me as to what I am to do along the way. I am ready, I am ready, I am ready. It is done, it is done, it is done and so it is. Thank you, thank you, thank you.'*

Then you must fold the paper up and put it away somewhere precious and safe. Don't read it again; trust that it is underway.

This is the key. Trust and be unwavering in your belief.

One small caveat: be careful what you ask for. I asked for someone who would challenge me. By May 2007, I met my lovely now husband Garrett, and while all the physical attributes manifested, he has also challenged me from day one! Don't get me wrong; it's a good thing. He teaches me about myself more than anyone else could have, he has also taught me patience and has helped me to love myself more than ever. We have shared values, shared love and I learn from this relationship every day. When my buttons are pushed, I see it as an opportunity to look within, to look at what is pushing those buttons and take responsibility for how I respond.

Improved existing relationship

All relationships require some sort of work over time. We are all evolving and changing and so are our partners, so it's important that we give our relationships space to grow, heal and be nurtured. A great way to keep your relationship strong, loving and fulfilled through the changing times is to actively choose it.

Try this mantra if you're in an existing relationship: 'I choose for my relationship with my husband, wife or partner to be loving, joyous and fulfilling.'

Bring your awareness to your heart. Imagine your partner. Feel the love in your heart for your partner. Now allow your heart to connect to their heart. Feel, imagine, see and sense the love that runs between you. From that place of love start imagining your relationship as you would love it to be – the laughter, the fun, the connection, the things that you do together, your interactions together, the communication, the intimacy, the joy and the shared values. Imagine your experiences together. Allow the love to be felt and expanded from your heart to theirs; imagine, sense or feel the love coming right back to you. Then write as much as possible in your journal. Keep on writing until you feel complete. Read what you received; is there more to be added?

Ask your heart: 'How many actions are there to take to keep me aligned to my beautiful relationship?'

Some things that Garrett and I do to ensure we are staying aligned are:

⇒ We have a date night booked in each week; sometimes we go out, sometimes it's just dinner at home, but we always give ourselves time together to eat at the table with TV and phones off so we can catch up properly.

⇒ Each evening we practice gratitude and share this with each other.

⇒ We have a rule that if we have a disagreement or a fight that we must resolve it before we go to bed.

Relationships take work to keep them fresh. Maintaining your connection to what you want is important, rather than focusing on what might be wrong.

Beware the rising ego

Regardless of what you're manifesting, watch out for the ego! It will rear its head and resistance will make itself known. We generally feel resistance in our bodies, so when you do, you might like to try the exercise below that I use with my clients to great benefit.

With the vision of what you want to create in mind, ask yourself:

> *Are there any doubts, fears or resistance? If so, what are they? How does it feel? Is there any disbelief, anger, annoyance or fear? Really let yourself feel what's going on. When you feel these feelings, can you feel them in your body? If so, where? What is the feeling? What does it look like? If it had a colour, what would it be? If it had a shape, what would it be? If it had a texture what would that be? If it had a temperature, what would that be?*

Now rate it for intensity out of ten, ten being almost unbearable zero being nothing. Once you have the rating, you've faced into what's going on and you have a starting point for improvement.

Next comes the opportunity to release the resistance. A way to release it is to imagine a glass bowl in front of you, and, with the power of intention and imagination, ask the resistance to be released into the bowl. Ask it to be released and be gone from your body. Release, release, release. Check to see that it has been released. Is it in the bowl? Is it moving? If so, it's now time to dissolve it. You get to dissolve it by asking it to spin either clockwise or anti-clockwise. As it spins, imagine it being sucked up to the light, completely dissolving and disintegrating. Keep going until there is nothing left in the bowl. Then go back to your body to check in and see if there is any remaining resistance, doubts or fear sitting in your body. If so, rate it out of ten and repeat the process.

Then ask yourself again: 'Am I truly aligned to my vision?' If the answer is 'yes', you are ready. You are aligned and you are unwavering. Your vision is ready to be manifested.

In the next chapter we'll explore how to take this vision and turn it into inspired action. This is where it starts to get real. Nothing will happen unless you take the steps to make it happen.

Let's recap the process:

1. Make your intention clear using an 'I am' or 'I choose' statement. An alternative statement to use is: 'For my highest good …', or 'For the highest good of all …'

2. Bring your awareness to your heart and feel, sense, see or hear what is in your heart in relation to your intention. Visualise and imagine what your intention would be like. Allow your heart to guide you, feel the love in your heart for what you're intending.

3. Write out as much as you can, then read it back. Expand on it. How does it make you feel? Is there more to add?

4. Are there any doubts, fears, disbelief or feelings of unworthiness? Feel into your body where that is. Feel it, sense it, explore it and face into it as much as possible.

5. Try releasing any negativity by using the imaginary bowl exercise.

6. Check in and ask: 'Am I unwavering with my intention? Do I truly believe that it will happen?'

7. Time to get your inspired actions in line. Ask your heart, 'How many inspired actions are there for me to take?' List them out.

8. Now you're ready to take action.

The following is an example of intention and vision:

My client Grant started working with me early in 2018. He is a successful property developer and the work we were initially going to do was helping him grow his business and staying in the flow. However, as our time together progressed it became apparent that he was not happy in his personal life. Grant is a gay man who came to terms with his sexuality later in life. He was in a hidden relationship with another man that had been going on for three years, however he wasn't out due to his fear of the reaction of his family, his old friends and as his business colleagues.

He was essentially living two lives: his authentic life with his boyfriend and the circle of friends he was socialising with. His family, business colleagues and old friends had no idea what was really going on in his other hidden life. He wasn't happy with his weight, his health and he was drinking and taking drugs excessively to mask a major problem in his life.

We started exploring what it would look and be like to be authentic to himself, his family and friends and what would it be like to 100 per cent love and accept himself for who he is as a gay man.

That was the starting point and through our work together through one-on-one coaching and Grant attending our retreats. He started to open up. He progressively began to love, appreciate and fully accept who he is both for his accomplishments and his wonderful relationship with his partner. He also came to the realisation that he had been inauthentic to himself. He started making healthy choices, exercising, drinking less and he quit taking drugs. He started feeling really good about himself. From that shift and allowing the space to be himself, he realised he was ready to share his truth and true self with his business colleagues, then his closest old schoolfriend. He felt so much better, and what he experienced was total acceptance by everyone he told.

He was actually surprised how easy it was. As our work progressed the space was opening up and he felt he was ready to tell his siblings, but he had concerns as his family was quite conservative and from regional New Zealand. He was also considering telling his mum, but he had no intention of telling his conservative dad. Otherwise, he knew he was ready to begin. First, he told his brother, who was very accepting of Grant. Then he was ready to tell his mum. She said, 'As my son, no matter what, I love you.' This was all coinciding with a family gathering, where he was then able to tell the rest of his family. He never told his dad, but his mum had in fact told her husband. While his dad didn't really understand, he was reflective on it.

Fast forward to today, Grant's partner is now totally accepted into the family and they stay at his parents as a couple. Grant now has much deeper loving relationships with his family and with his partner, Vinny. They will both spend the first Christmas with Grant's family to the excitement of everyone involved.

Chapter Five

Taking Inspired Action

We've talked about creating your vision and getting connected and focused on what you want. Now it's time to bring your vision into reality, and the way to do that is to take action. Inspired action. Nothing will manifest without taking some sort of action. You must *do something* to move towards what you desire.

Inspired action versus action

So, what exactly is 'inspired action' as opposed to normal everyday action? Rational, forced or 'normal' action is the type of action you take just because that's what others have done. It might be a rational approach, or it could just be for the sake of it. It could be when your mind is clouded and you're coming from a place of reaction or fear, and the action taken is a result of feeling like something has to be done. This 'forced action' comes from a place of lack and limitation, not from a place of ease or alignment to your outcome.

Of course, rational action absolutely has its place. Take brushing your teeth, for example. You know it must be done and rationally how to do it and when to do it. It doesn't need to be an inspired action. The same goes for driving a car to get somewhere. You rationally know you need to get from point A to point B, the route you must take and how to operate the car.

Inspired action is very different. It's taking steps that come from your intuition, your own inner guidance system. It's action from the heart, your internal knowing, your gut feeling. It's when you just know, even when your ego (your limited self) might not want you to.

Inspired action is powerful. It can lead you to faster results in a relatively short timeframe and in some instances with immediate outcomes. Often an inspired action is a shift in mindset; from resistance and thoughts of lack, to shifting your thoughts to exactly what you wish to manifest in the moment.

To maximise the potential of inspired action taking, you must always have a clear outcome in your mind's eye that you're moving towards. The more unwavering you are in the vision of your outcome, the clearer and more aligned the necessary inspired actions will be.

Inspired action is where the magic happens

I want to tell you about Harry. Harry was out racing his MINI at a race day in the outer suburbs of Melbourne. It's a hobby he loves, and it gives him great joy. One particular day he pushed the car really hard, so much that he blew the engine up. In that moment he had two choices. He could either get upset about the car blowing up or not. Consciously, he knew that the incident was a very real possibility in the car racing experience and what he had to deal with next was the practicality of the situation. He had driven the car to the event, some distance out of Melbourne, and somehow needed to get himself and the car back home. What Harry chose instead of panic or anger was to keep his cool and be relaxed, knowing that it would work out.

Before calling a tow truck he noticed that there was a truck parked at the event. His inspired action was to find the truck driver and see if he was able to drop him and the car home. Sure enough, the truckie had no return vehicle booked in to take back and was only too happy to help Harry out; even more conveniently, it was actually on his way home. Harry took the action of finding the driver and the rest worked itself out. He didn't stress and he was in a place of trusting and allowing. From that place, an almost instant solution availed itself. Like magic!

Let me share another recent story to illustrate inspired action. I was on a facilitated weekend silent meditation retreat as a participant and I was there to fully embrace the silence and the opportunity to go deep within myself. On day two in meditation I was receiving clear intuitive guidance that I was to tell the facilitator that I channel sound, and that I was to offer to lead a channelled, guided meditation. When I thought about it consciously, I didn't want to actually do it. I didn't want to be leading anything, let alone a channelled sound meditation. In my mind I was there just to go within and receive. But I kept receiving this particular guidance, so I said to the universe,

'Okay, if it's true for me to offer this to the facilitator then I need a clear sign,' and I told the universe the sign must be a white feather.

That afternoon the facilitator led us on a walking meditation outside and within five minutes there was a white feather on the ground in clear view to me. So, of course, I had to tell him. I took the inspired action. As it turned out, due to the event being tightly scheduled there wasn't an opportunity for me to lead a meditation. Regardless, we had a great conversation and I'm glad I spoke up. The experience reminded me to always follow my own inner guidance – even when I might not want to – because then it will always lead me somewhere.

The other lesson in this story is that there is great power in asking the universe for a sign to reiterate a request, especially when it's something our ego doesn't want us to do. A sign or symbol can help clarify the path forward or provide confirmation that you're on the right track.

Let's relate this to your Land of Abundance. Your Land of Abundance is your big picture vision; it's something that will unfold over many years.

When you're working towards big goals, keep aligning and connecting to them and then checking in on yourself. Ask, 'What will I do today to move myself forward? What's an inspiring action to take that's right in front of me now?' Usually, inspired actions are just small steps, but it's from those small steps that more will be shown to you. The opportunities will avail themselves; the right people will show up and the right information will avail itself. Keep following what's in front of you, what feels good, what feels aligned and before you know it your Land of Abundance will unfold before your eyes.

Tapping into your intuition for guidance

I find the most effective way to know what inspired action to take is to first deeply connect into what you want to manifest or create. Perhaps read what you wrote about your Land of Abundance, your affirmation statements or look at your vision board for a few minutes. Another way is through breathing with an intention; put your hand on your heart and ask, 'Is it in my truth to do...?'

'How many inspired actions am I to take today to move me forward?' You will always get the answer. Once you have the answer, tune in and ask, 'What is the number one thing I need to do?' If you get stuck remember to drink water – this frees up the mind and the energy. Why not give it a go right now?

You might also get your inspired actions from being in particular places, such as in the shower or out in nature – anywhere that allows you to have the space to be completely present.

Wherever and however that looks for you is fine. I know one of my clients gets lots of inspired ideas and actions when she's gardening. For another client, driving creates the necessary space, especially on long road trips.

Muscle testing for answers

If you're struggling to tap into your inspired action through your intuition, you might like to use a more physical methodology. Our bodies are very clever! They give us answers to all sorts of questions through muscle testing or applied kinesiology, as it's scientifically known.

Your body gives you a 'yes' or 'no' response, providing that the question you're asking it is a question for your highest good. Inside and surrounding your body is an electrical network or grid. This is pure energy. Because energy runs through the muscles in your body, if anything impacts your electrical system that doesn't maintain or enhance your body's balance, your muscles will virtually 'short circuit' or weaken (don't worry, it's only temporary).

Things that might have an impact on your electrical system are thoughts, emotions, foods and other substances. Using your muscles, you can locate what events or emotions weaken or strengthen your body. This muscle testing process is an excellent way to clarify answers to some big questions; it's a bit like a messenger to your subconscious mind.

Try a simple muscle testing technique on yourself now – the sway test. It might take some practice to get real accuracy and consistency but keep at it and you'll find a whole new way of communicating with your body.

1. Stand or sit up straight with your feet pointing directly forward. Make sure both feet are facing forwards, and that neither foot is slightly turned in nor out. Relax your body with your hands down at your sides.

2. To ensure your energy is running in a forward direction (which helps provide an accurate result), tap your thymus gland. This is under your breast bone in your chest – about an inch below

the notch in your neck where you'd tie a tie. Simply tap there for about thirty seconds. You don't need to be perfectly on the spot, as the percussive effect of the tapping will do the work.

3. Now you're ready to perform an accuracy check. To make sure you're getting an accurate response, make a statement or hold a thought in your head that you know is true. For example, *My name is [insert your own name]*. Then state something false like, *My name is [insert someone else's name]*. Sense the response of your body for each answer — you should feel yourself being gently pulled forward for a 'yes' response or repelled back for a 'no', signalling the statement either is or isn't in resonance with you.

4. Now you can begin asking other questions using this method.

Some examples of the way you might ask questions related to your emotions would be:

⇒ 'Am I feeling upset because of a work situation?' If you answer yes, then you can continue asking more specific questions.

⇒ 'Am I feeling upset because of something person X said to me?'

⇒ 'Would it be beneficial for me to talk to person X to clarify this issue?'

⇒ 'Is it in my truth and for my highest good to work with this person?'

If you aren't getting a perceptible response with the sway test, you might prefer to try an alternative muscle testing technique. Make an okay symbol by making a circle with your first finger and thumb of both hands and letting the other fingers point straight. Do this with both hands and interlink them. Breathe deeply, evenly and calmly. Place your feet firmly on the floor with your legs uncrossed. This will help you get an accurate result. When you ask a question that can be answered with a 'yes' or 'no' response, you're going to pull the fingers against each other. If the link holds strong, that is a 'yes' answer. If the link breaks easily, the answer is 'no'.

Pendulum for answers

Pendulums are often used as tools for spiritual healing and inner growth as well as guidance, such as seeking your inspired actions. Pendulums are objects attached at the end of a string or metal chain, which, when suspended from a stationary position, will swing back and forth or in a circular motion. Pendulums are made from a variety of materials including crystals, wood, glass and metals.

Understand the directional swings

Pendulums swing in vertical straight lines, horizontal straight lines and in circular movements. This can be done side-by-side, front and back, clockwise, counter-clockwise, in an elliptical motion, or even in a bobbing motion and up and down.

Define the directional swings

Before you begin to ask questions, you must first assign each directional swing a response. You do this by asking the pendulum to show you what certain responses look like. For example, start off by asking, 'What does a no look like?' and then, 'What does a yes look like?' Posing these questions to your pendulum will help define directional swings, which must happen before advancing to more challenging questions.

Pendulum response examples

⇒ Vertical swing signifies no

⇒ Horizontal swing signifies yes

⇒ Circular movement is neutral

Prepare your questions

It's important that your question can be answered with a positive, negative or neutral response.

Some good question examples might be:

1. Is it in my truth and for my highest good to ask about my job interview?
2. Will I be offered the job I interviewed for this morning?

Examples of poor questions are:

1. Should I get a black or silver Mercedes?
2. Will my pregnant sister have a boy or girl?

Set intentions

It's imperative to precede the question session with a request or statement. For example: 'Is it in my truth and for the highest good to ask about ...'

Questions to ask before and between the next

Be prepared to ask several questions in order to receive enough information to get to your answer. Make sure to completely stop any pendulum motion between questions to clear any lingering energies that relate to the previous question. Accept information only if your intuition assures you it's accurate.

Next time you aren't sure of what step to take, try one of these techniques and see if you can get clear answers.

A daily practice

My most productive and powerful days are those when I create space to tune into what my inspired actions will be for that day. It makes a big difference to spend a little time each day doing this, as it inevitably saves me loads of time because I'm not spending energy on the wrong things! When clients work with me, we always tune into what inspired actions ought to be taken between our sessions.

Here's the catch. Just because I write the actions down doesn't mean that they all get done. Nothing is going to be done just because I write it down. I actually have to physically take the action. Take writing this book for example. I made a commitment with my book coach (yes, I have one to guide me and help keep me accountable) to do some work on my book each day, and because I made that commitment it bugged me until I took action. Some days the action is big, others it's very small, but as long as I'm doing something towards keeping that commitment, the project moves forward.

If you're anything like me, there will be certain things that are effortless to do and others that get put off. I particularly put off the creative things like writing. I procrastinate and delay and come up with all manner of excuses. You see, it's my ego at play; my ego which comes from fear; fear of my greatness and fear of failing at the creation. It's resistance and attachment at play. The key is to first acknowledge the ego (your limited self) with compassion and push forward. Just as I have done to complete this book.

In the example of writing this book, it simply comes down to me putting my fingers on the keyboard and creating the space to take the action. The pure act of doing so opens up the creative flow and opens me up to the universe's support with the creation. The momentum begins.

Sometimes the action can be really scary; sometimes it might not be comfortable to do. For instance, you may know you need to leave a relationship, a job or a city, but these are massive steps! You always have free will, but, if the requirement to move is true, you will keep getting the nudges, the signs and the reasons, and you must trust that even when it's hard and when that real leap of faith is required, you will be okay. It might not feel like it at the time, but you need to trust that you'll be fine. Remember to be kind to yourself and ask the universe for support to help you make the transition with as much ease and grace as possible. However, with that said, sometimes we just have to do the work and be brutally honest about getting unstuck to move forward.

The same goes with anything you get the inspiration to do. It's so important to take the action, even if it appears small or insignificant, because it's the small steps that lead you to where you're meant to go – to the greater and more abundant you. Notice where you have resistance, acknowledge it and push through. That's when the momentum begins, inspiration occurs, external support appears, and it all starts to unfold. Before you know it, you've completed your creation and your vision has revealed itself.

No results? Check for truth

A common trap for those new to this process is that when you have taken some sort of action and you aren't seeing results or outcomes immediately, you give up. That's the ego at play again. This is the time you need to reconnect with your vision and your intention, and ask yourself, 'Is this still true for me?'

If you're still answering 'yes', ask yourself, 'Am I attached to it appearing in a certain timeframe or in a certain way?' Check in with how you're feeling. Are you sensing lack and limitation? Are you feeling a distrust that it will come? Are there any remaining doubts or even feelings of unworthiness present? Ask yourself, 'Do I feel good? Do I feel aligned? Am I 100 per cent trusting that this or something even better is unfolding?'

Here's the challenge – what you thought you were working towards might actually be a stepping stone to something far greater than you could have conceptualised, which is why it's not showing up as you had hoped. Timing may also be an issue – if you're working on drawing in another person, it might not be the right time or for the highest alignment for them.

Remember this: your manifestations, your dreams, your visions will not happen without taking deliberate and inspired action.

Let me share about my client Anna. Anna is a real estate agent, she is also the mother four children as well as four step-children. As you can imagine, she's pretty busy. I've been working with her for almost two years and during our sessions we usually have at 6 am as that's the only time she has.

What I love about working with her is that she creates a space with me that helps her keep aligned to her power and to her light. The other day we were in session and she said to me, 'Jason, you know what? I'm in the attractor business.' And she is exactly right.

Her most important action she takes is to keep her vibration as an attractor. This means that she is aligned to drawing in new listings, buyers and solutions and she inherently knows that it will all fall into place. And it does. Yes, she does the work, but her primary work is keeping her vibration high. She meditates, practises gratitude, visits her vision portfolio morning and night, and keeps her awareness on how she shows up.

This year Anna was named 76th top agent within Australia and in the top ten female agents for McGrath, all of this while being an amazing mum, wife, daughter and community member. She is such a joy to work with.

Chapter Six

Harnessing the Universe to Support You

The universe, God, source, your higher self, the divine, law of nature … however you wish to refer to it is absolutely fine. If you have religious beliefs, then that's also good. Call on your God and refer to the universe I speak of here as your God.

Many of the teachings I discuss in this book are actually in the Bible and other religious texts. Sadly, they're often not written in comprehensible ways. In this chapter, as I have said in the previous chapters, I reference as the universe.

The universe wants to support you to have an abundant life; to live to the fullest expression of yourself and to lead a life filled with joy and expansion. We all came here with great purpose, and we came to expand into the fullness of ourselves, but we also came here forgetting who we truly are and how powerful we actually are.

It's only our minds or often referred to as our ego that creates limitations, fears and attachments. These lead us to believe that we're separate from each other, when we're actually all connected. When we think of ourselves as separate, we actually block our true connection to all that is.

It's our minds that make us believe that we're not capable or powerful, and that if we can't see something with our eyes, then it's not real. But let's challenge this for a moment. You can't see electricity, heat or radio and Wi-Fi frequencies – yet we know that they're real. Why are we happy to believe in them but so many of us struggle to believe in a God or higher being? We're all connected energetically and when you can accept this then learn to harness it, you become very powerful. Essentially, you harness the universe to manifest what you would love.

Let's look to nature for an example. If you can, look at a tree right now. No matter what's happening, that tree remains as it is, it doesn't react, and it doesn't resist or attach. It remains completely present to whatever happens, whether it's being blown around in a storm or birds are nesting in it or if it's a glorious sunny day and it stands still. Even if its limbs are being removed it remains. That is the law of nature. Nature carries on no matter what. It might need to adjust but it doesn't complain, it just gets on and finds a way forward.

It's in our humanness to have certain beliefs and to operate certain ways based on our life experiences, our upbringing as well as our own perceptions. We often crave an outcome, or we have an aversion to what is appearing in our life experiences, and we resist. But you can harness the law of nature (the universe) by actually trusting and allowing that all is unfolding in its natural order and for the highest outcome for all.

As I said in Chapter One, there is always an opportunity to harness the laws of the universe and to work with it. Remember, what you focus on creates your reality, because that is the frequency or energy that you're emitting. So, always have a clear intention and keep your focus on what you want to bring forth, then ask the universe to support you with it.

If you can trust and know that what you're asking for is underway, you can keep your awareness on the actions you must take, which then leads to what you wish for. The better you feel about what you're drawing forth, and as if it's already happened, the easier it will be.

So, how can you harness the universe to support you? The first thing is to always have a crystal-clear intention. Ask yourself, 'What am I wishing to bring forth, to create, to manifest? Is it for my highest good? Is it for the highest good of all?' The most powerful way to do this is by connecting with your heart. Try this now. Put your hand on your heart. Feel, sense or imagine the energy from your heart and ask your heart to open up. Say, 'Hello, heart, I love you, I love you.' Feel it, sense it and imagine it opening up even more. Then ask your heart about your intention; you will most probably feel a lightness and an openness if your intention is true for you. You may even see, sense or feel your intention from an expanded perspective.

Once you have that clear intention you must fully believe in it, be unwavering in this belief and be fully worthy of it. Again, put your hand on your heart and ask your heart: 'Are there any doubts?' If there is any doubt you will feel it. If there are any feelings of unworthiness or limiting beliefs going on, then these need to be cleared first. Bring your awareness to those doubts and ask yourself: 'Is this true?' Are there any feelings of fear or any resistance in your body? If so, go into that feeling and sit with it until it subsides. Once you feel neutral, aligned and open in your heart, then you're ready to harness the universe for support.

By facing your doubts, your fears and your resistance, you start creating space to heal and to move through whatever is blocking you. We can't remove our fears or our blocks without facing them first. If you don't face your fears or blocks, they will keep showing up. This is the law of what you resist persists.

Make no mistake, at times your mind is going to think that this is crazy stuff. It's important to acknowledge that while it's hard to comprehend this process from the rational mind, it's okay. The more you have faith and trust, the more you open yourself up to this expanded field of opportunity and possibility.

When you're aligned the universe will support you. Know that you don't have to do it all by yourself! I've experienced this firsthand, and I've witnessed it with so many people. You might have heard the quote, 'Ask and you shall receive, ask and it is given.' Well, it's true. The universe responds to your request when you're trusting and in true alignment, so ask away.

I'll share with you an example. I've recently repackaged my coaching program and pricing and I was ready to manifest new clients. The first thing I did was check in using my heart and my intuition, regarding whether I believed 100 per cent in my abilities and myself. The answer was yes. Then I questioned whether I believed 100 per cent in my pricing, value and my offerings.

Again, a yes. I felt no resistance, no doubt. I felt openness in my heart. I asked, 'Are my offerings for my highest good and for the highest good of all?' Yes, my heart was open, and I felt aligned. Then I knew I was ready to harness the universe to support me.

Here's a script or mantra you might like to borrow and adapt for your own situation:

> *'Universe, I am clear on my new offerings and I am ready for my new clients to come forth to take up these offerings. Please send me my ideal paying clients now. I am ready, and I am grateful to be working with these new clients. Please show me the signs that I'm on track. Thank you, thank you, thank you. It is done.'*

The signs I usually see are 11:11 1:01 3:33 4:44 usually on my phone, also on number plates as well as unexpected places. But yours could be anything you choose. It might be feathers, a particular animal or insect. Choose whatever resonates with you.

Starter exercise

The following exercise is a fun way to test out this idea of getting support from the universe.

1. First bring awareness to your heart.

2. Put your hand on your heart and say, 'Heart, I love you.' Feel your heart open.

3. From that openness in your heart, say, 'Dear universe, please send me a surprise or a gift within the next forty-eight hours. Thank you, thank you, thank you. It is done.'

4. Then let it go. Trust and know inherently that a surprise or gift is on its way to you.

In action

I asked the universe recently for some help. We were in the process of settling on an investment property and, as it's an investment property, we needed a bank loan for it. This particular property was purchased off the plan and during the time it took to be built (it was way over schedule) the property market dropped and then only somewhat recovered. To minimise how much money we had to put into the deal we needed the bank to value the property at the purchase price or more. I knew that I needed to have the intention that it would all work out perfectly, and I kept myself in that mindset.

In my morning meditation I would send feelings of appreciation to this property and gratitude for the excellent investment that it was. When the valuer was booked, I started sending love to the valuer and I asked the universe to pave the way for the property to be valued up to or more than the purchase price. Then I let it go and trusted inherently that it was underway. Sure enough, the valuation was on the exact contract price.

Let me now share a story about my client, David, working with the universe. Each year David and his mates booked the same beautiful property up in the Byron Bay hinterland for the week over New Year. He absolutely loved this property. When we started working together, as I do with all my clients, I got him to vision out his Land of Abundance. One of the things he visualised was owning a beautiful property up in Byron Bay much like the one he stayed at each year.

As our work progressed, out of the blue a real estate agent contacted him with an offer from a commercial client interested in his Sydney property. As David looked into the offer it became clear that it could be a very lucrative proposition. The negotiation process resulted in a significant price for his property, as a developer wanted to turn it into apartments. It also meant that he could stay living there, paying nominal rent until they were ready to develop it. Suddenly, the idea of buying a property up in Byron Bay was very much within reach. He had an inspired idea to reach out to the owners of the property he rented each year; amazingly, just that week, they were talking about downsizing.

He asked the universe for support if it was for the highest good to have it all unfold effortlessly and, sure enough, he was able to negotiate an off-market purchase. He now owns the property, debt free, and has it leased out when he's not using it. It has turned out to be a very lucrative investment and is a beautiful sanctuary for him to visit many times throughout the year.

Wonderfully for me, the Byron Bay property is where we hold our November retreats, so I can attest to its beauty and special feel. What I love about this experience for David is that he couldn't have planned the whole thing if he'd tried! He was simply totally in alignment; the property gave him joy every time he went there and every time he thought about it. He allowed it to unfold, so it did.

Ease and divine timing experiment

An easy way to test out the support of the universe is when you're planning a trip, or already en route, and you want to arrive at your destination with ease and in divine timing. I use this all the time, particularly when driving in Sydney where the traffic can be very unpredictable. Try saying this: 'universe, please help me pave the way to get to my destination with ease and in divine timing.' Trust it is done and follow your inner guidance system. Notice the ease with which you then travel. It works every time if you truly believe it and allow it. You will get in the fastest lanes, the lights will be in your favour, and you'll know that if there are any delays, you're still being lined up to get where you need to go in divine timing.

Heart to heart

Connecting your heart to another's heart is very powerful in providing support for your desires. Our hearts emit a frequency and the more open our hearts are the happier and lighter we feel. When we consciously send love from our heart to another's, we send out the highest vibration of all. The recipient might not necessarily feel it, but energetically there is a connection happening. Try it out for fun and notice how people react in response to this. As a daily practice in meditation you may like to send love from your heart to another's.

To do this, bring your awareness to them and to your heart, then feel the love in your heart for that person and send it out. It's very powerful and feels really lovely. Try it out on projects you are working on too. This morning in meditation I sent love to my book, to pave the way for the words to come easily.

Experiment with this. It's okay if you don't get it right every time. Your mind is going to step up and offer doubt and disbelief. Just know that it's part of the process. Love and accept that part of you and keep going. Keep playing and having fun with it.

Sometimes you might ask for something and it's just not happening. Try not to be disheartened. As mentioned earlier, there are a number of reasons this could be happening. The first is that there is always a higher plan going on and more often than not we aren't yet aware of that higher plan. Secondly, there might be lessons to be had from what is actually showing up. Are you allowing yourself to see what those lessons are? Also, remember, everything happens in divine timing; there is always something greater available to you if you will allow it. Finally, remember to check in with yourself to see if you're attached to the outcome or pushing it away. Are you truly allowing it?

The most important thing is to keep feeling good about and grateful for what already is. The more you come from this place of gratitude, the more the good will be shown to you. Have faith and know that you don't have to do this alone. Call on the support that is available to you. You are worthy of this amazing and abundant life.

Chapter Seven

Resistance & Attachment

This chapter contains the information that's the most important for you to master. However, the concepts here are also often the most challenging to break through. We're talking about resistance and attachment. Without releasing these, you will struggle to vibrationally align to your vision and therefore you won't manifest your desires.

I'm going to answer the following questions for you, so I can help you move through these states easily.

1. What is resistance?

2. What is attachment?

3. What is vibration?

4. How do you know if you are in resistance or attachment?

5. Why do you need to overcome resistance and attachment for the Law of Attraction to work?

How do you move into a state of trusting and allowing for your manifestations to come forth?

Let's say that you have clarity about what your Land of Abundance looks and feels like. You're really clear on what you would love to create in your life. You've visualised and connected to your heart with what you truly want, and you've seen it as your most expansive self. You have a clear vision.

Now it's time to manifest this vision, this Land of Abundance. Unfortunately, what typically happens is that as soon as you start moving towards your vision, your limited thoughts and feelings start to show themselves. They either show up as resistance or as attachment, meaning you will either be pushing away what you want because of fears and limiting beliefs about yourself or others, or your mind will be making it a matter of life and death. You'll limit your Land of Abundance by believing it must show up in a specific way or in a specific timeframe; you'll be too invested in the outcome.

Put simply, *resistance* is when you oppose what you truly want, usually because fear of some sort is present. Whereas, *attachment* is when you desperately crave your outcome and you're fixated on what you want coming to you in a certain way and in a certain timeframe.

When we really want something, it can feel impossible to then surrender it. If you've done work around clarifying your desire and visualising it, how can you just detach from it?

The answer is practise. Detaching from outcomes isn't easy. It doesn't necessarily come naturally, especially when the outcome is something we desperately want. But you can get better at this detachment process by bringing your awareness to it.

Detaching from an outcome doesn't mean you don't take action. In fact, the opposite is true. You do take action, but you take it from a place of absolute belief; the more unwavering you are with your belief the easier it will be to draw forth what you desire. You wholeheartedly trust that the universe will give you whatever is of the highest good for you, even if it's not exactly what you planned or thought you wanted.

Become a vibrational match to your vision

To manifest you must move into a state of complete trust and allowing. You must be unwavering in your belief that your vision will happen in perfect timing and better than expected. You must be a complete vibrational match to what you wish to draw forth as if it's already happened.

Whenever your intention fails to manifest, no matter what it is, it means that you're out of alignment in some way and that you're not a vibrational match with what you're trying to manifest.

Why is this so?

Everything is vibration or energy. Everything is energetically- or vibrationally-based. Think about sound, for example. If you hear music with a loud bass, you can feel the vibration of that sound. Whenever you hear something, you're interpreting the vibration; what you hear is the interpretation of the sound. Each of your physical senses of seeing, hearing, tasting, smelling and touching exist because everything in the universe is vibrating, and your physical senses are picking up on the vibrations or the energy to give you the sensory perception.

> 'Everything that exists, in your air, in your dirt, in your water and in your bodies, is vibration in motion – and all of it is managed by the powerful Law of Attraction. When you ask for the manifestation prior to the vibration, you ask the impossible. When you are willing to offer the vibration before the manifestation, all things are possible. It is Law.'

So how do you know if you're out of alignment and in resistance or attachment?

The quickest way to know is through how you feel. Do you feel the lack of what you wish for, do your thoughts feel good? If your thoughts are positive and those thoughts make you feel good, then you're aligned. From that good feeling you then have access to another good feeling and then another and another. Before you know it, you've moved into a very high frequency state, one that allows for more good feelings and experiences.

But if you're coming from a place of lack, then the universe will respond with same frequency or vibration that you're putting out. *As Abraham Hicks says, 'The essence of that which is like unto itself is drawn.' What that means is if I feel that I'm lacking, and I keep repeating negative thoughts and keep having negative conversations around money, the Law of Attraction can't now surround me with money, as that would defy the Law of Attraction.

This is why it's so important to reach for what feels good and for what is abundant.

*Abraham Hicks is channelled information from source energy, specifically around the teachings of Law of Attraction. Abraham is channelled by Esther Hicks.

If you're coming from a place of reaching for what you love, for what gives you pleasure and reaching for those good feeling thoughts, then you're in a frequency of abundance and of drawing forth your manifestation.

When you become aware of being out of alignment and you're conscious of the negative thoughts and feelings dominating your choices, you can choose to reach for a good feeling thought to turn things around. It doesn't matter what it is, as long as it makes you feel better and you can start moving yourself back into alignment.

Abraham calls this 'pivoting'. Ask yourself: 'What thoughts can I reach for in this very moment? What do I want? What do I really want? What is it that I'm choosing in this moment?'

Another way to pivot is to use affirmations. You can reframe your thoughts immediately by having your affirmations ready to go. Revisiting your Land of Abundance, your visions and your vision board and listening to your first-person recordings are also ways to help realign you back into flow.

Meditation is another a very important ingredient in this recalibration process. The more you create space through meditation, the more you have access to your intuitive self and to the steps that are available for you to take at any time. It will bring your energy back into the frequency of flow and will help you connect with your heart.

Whenever you feel dissatisfied, fearful, demotivated or in reaction to something or someone, that's your opportunity to inquire with yourself about what's really going on. 'What am I thinking about? Am I thinking about what I don't want?' Accept the feeling rather than judge yourself for it, then use the opportunity to reach for a better feeling or thought.

What do you want? What do you love? What can you see in front of you? When you consciously do that, you keep yourself aligned to what it is that you truly want.

Let me give you an example.

One of my clients has a large engineering business and he came to me because he wasn't making a profit at the time. As we worked together, it became very clear that he was focused on all the things going wrong in his business. Whenever anyone made a mistake, he felt personally responsible for it, and so that's where his focus was. He lost sight of the business being profitable and was unmotivated, and he always concentrated on the negatives.

For him to turn the business around he needed to realise and then own the fact that he was focusing on all the negatives. That was his starting point.

From there, he needed to clarify what he really wanted to create in his business: happy customers, a joyful team, a feeling of belief in his business and, of course, making a profit. Every time we had a session, I asked him to tune into what his next steps were. Though previously he had felt confused about what to do next, he suddenly felt as if he always had the answers; importantly, he always took the action. As a result, he turned his business around and it's become very successful and profitable since.

Tap your way to balance

Another handy tool that I use on myself and with clients is Emotional Freedom Technique (EFT) or tapping. I've taken Gabrielle Bernstein's (another of my wonderful teachers) excellent explanation of it from her book *Judgement Detox*:

> *'EFT is a psychological acupressure technique that supports your emotional health. EFT is unique in bringing together the cognitive benefits of therapy with the physical benefits of acupuncture to restore your energy and heal your emotions. EFT does not use needles. You simply stimulate certain meridian points on the body by tapping on them with your fingertips.*

More than five thousand years ago, the Chinese recognised a series of energy circuits that run through the body. They call these circuits *meridians*, and today this concept is the basis for acupuncture and acupressure healing. When you tap on specific energy meridians found on your face, head, arm, and chest, you can release old fears, limiting beliefs, negative patterns, and even physical pain. While you tap, you talk out loud about the issue you are working to heal. Allowing yourself to emote while simultaneously tapping on the energy points sends a signal to the brain that it's safe to relax. Our fear response, which is controlled by the amygdala, is lessened.

The goal of EFT is to balance disturbances in your energy field, not unearth any specific memory. Great healing and relief can come without having to relive any memories at all.

Gary Craig, who created EFT, has said, 'The cause of all negative emotions is a disruption in the body's energy system.' Gary believes that the negative emotion is not caused by a traumatic memory or experience; it's caused by a traumatic event that *creates a disruption in the body's energy system*. In turn, that disruption creates negative emotion. Through the process of EFT, you can heal the disruption in your energy system, thereby healing the emotions.

As Gary puts it:

> 'EFT operates on the premise that no matter what part of your life needs improvement, there are unresolved emotional issues in the way ... The EFT premise also includes the understanding that the more unresolved emotional issues you can clear, the more peace and emotional freedom you will have in your life ... With that in mind, EFT can be an ongoing process that we use to clear out the old traumas, and welcome any new challenges with a healthy, productive attitude.'

Let me share an example of how EFT worked to help heal one of my clients who suffered anxiety. Sharon works as a lawyer and is good at her job, but every so often she experienced anxiety. The problem was that she hated herself for it. The anxiety made her believe that she wasn't good enough or strong enough, and that she was a failure. So, I introduced Sharon to tapping. The simple process – that she could do alone, anywhere, anytime – not only helped her to accept the anxiety when it presented itself, but also allowed her to move the anxiety through her more effectively. She now very rarely experiences anxiety, but when she does, she has the tools to deal with it.

Another of my clients, Chloe, was addicted to Diet Coke. I asked her to hold the can of Diet Coke in her hand as she tapped. First, she had to accept the addiction. Only then was she able to reframe the addiction. After a few tapping sessions she is now completely free of her Diet Coke addiction. It's so simple, but so effective.

How do I know if I'm in resistance or attachment?

Now that you understand what resistance and attachment is, and how to move through it, you might be wondering what happens if you don't notice that you're experiencing resistance or attachment. The answer to that is quite simple. Wherever there is any negativity or dissatisfaction, fear or anger, you can be sure you have resistance or attachment.

You might also question what happens if you feel as though you can't break through resistance or attachment. Simply being aware of the fact that you're in resistance or attachment is a good starting point. From there, you need to be open to acknowledging and accepting the experience. The sooner you acknowledge the experience, the sooner you will move through it.

Resistance can often show up as illness or disease. Dis-ease.

Ways to release resistance or attachment

In summary, here is a list of ways to release your resistance or your attachment:

- ⇒ Meditation.
- ⇒ Tapping or EFT.

⇒ Bringing your awareness to the resistance. Where are you feeling it in your body? What does it feel like? What does it look like? What is the intensity of that? Feel it, accept it and love it as much as you can.

⇒ Reach for a positive-feeling thought. And then another. And then another.

⇒ Practising gratitude.

⇒ Go through your positive affirmations.

⇒ At the end of every day as you go to sleep, acknowledge the comfort of your bed, the health and wellbeing that runs through your body, the opportunities that have presented themselves to you and how delighted you are to be going into slumber.

⇒ On awakening, acknowledge the comfort of your bed, the sleep that you've had, the continued health and wellbeing that runs through your body and the healing that has occurred overnight as you slept and the excitement for the day and the opportunities that lie ahead.

The key is not to beat yourself up over resistance or attachment. Rather, realign and connect back into what you do want using one of the above practices. Move through the resistance and attachment and shift your focus on to your positive desires.

Keep yourself vibrationally aligned to your vision and before long it will manifest.

Chapter Eight

Purpose & Fulfillment

What is 'purpose'? What defines fulfillment and why should we be seeking it?

Life is about finding what gives us purpose and fulfillment. I firmly believe that we all came here with our own unique gifts and talents and that we all have a place in society to contribute these gifts and talents. These are the people who collect the rubbish because they enjoy having a positive impact on their community, to the bookkeeper who loves numbers and compliance, through to the molecular scientist who relishes the thrill of scientific discovery.

Most of us receive our greatest fulfillment from doing something for the greater good, something that benefits our community, society or our environment.

I also believe that as our lives progress, we evolve, and our purpose becomes more apparent. We have life experiences that take us on a journey, and while our journeys are all different, along the way most of us will experience exactly the opposite of what is purposeful to us. This is the universe's way of pointing out what *is* in fact purposeful. Abraham Hicks calls it *contrast*.

Key indicators of purpose

Throughout our lives we're offered key indicators of what we're meant to be doing with our lives. Usually it's the things that light us up and provide joy. They are also usually things we can do to serve others in some way.

When I reflect on what I was like as a child before my limiting beliefs were formed, some traits and behaviours are very clear. I know that I wanted to talk to everyone – strangers in the supermarket, people on the street, anyone and anywhere. I also loved cars and building Lego houses, cardboard houses and card houses. People interested me greatly, as did nice things.

So, it's interesting how my career has panned out: I first worked in insurance, sold cars and then real estate, but fundamentally it was my interest in people and my ability to read them which made me very good at sales and customer service. I inherently knew how to serve them.

As a coach that's also exactly what I do today. I am deeply interested in my clients and I innately know what's going on for them and how to best serve them. I only wish the best for those that I work with, as well as more broadly for my community and all of humanity.

Think about what you have been drawn to throughout your life. What did you play with as a child? How did you behave as a young child? What have you continually been attracted to throughout your life? There will be key indicators as to your purpose all along the way.

What moves you? What shakes you up? What pisses you off? What do you notice? What are you affected by? What lights you up? What are you good at? The more you bring your awareness to what you are affected by, good at, like and enjoy, the more you will become aware of what you are meant to be doing.

You might be thinking, *I could never make a living from what I love!* And that may very well be the case, so instead look at what you love doing as a tool or vehicle to help uncover more of what is purposeful for you.

I was recently interviewed for a podcast and the interviewer said that she loves dancing. She knows it's not something that she would do as a career, but it gives her absolute joy to dance around her house. That joy that she experiences as she dances brings her into a state of presence and from that state of presence and joy, she's putting out a frequency of joy. When she sets an intention before starting to dance, she's far more likely to bring forth that desire or answer because of the state of presence and joy that she is experiencing.

The same goes for someone that loves watching sport. You might not have the right physical form to be a footy player, but watching the game brings you into a state of presence – when you watch, there's nothing else going on other than that game. Try setting an intention before going in to watch a game, especially if you're looking for an answer to something. You'll usually have it come to you during the game because you've created space for presence. This is a great exercise to try out.

Being drawn to a particular form of sport is also a key indicator of purpose – ask yourself, 'Why do I enjoy it so much? What has drawn me to that, is it the physicality, the connection, the thrill of the game, the teamwork, the sense of community or is it the thrill of the competition? What do I see going on that perhaps others don't?'

Career fulfillment

According to a Gallup poll conducted during 2017, eighty-five per cent of workers actually hate their jobs. That is a huge and disturbing number. The exciting thing is that it doesn't have to be that way.

You can choose. You can choose to be dissatisfied or you can choose to take action and do something you would love that gives you joy.

It might be really scary to make a change, which is what puts you off doing it. I know when I've made career changes it's been scary. The most recent experience for me was when I decided to sell my real estate business to solely focus on coaching. It made no rational sense, as it was a financially abundant business and I still enjoyed it, but I knew that the time had come to fully commit to this next chapter in my life. I was fearful and I thought, *How could I possibly earn a decent living from coaching?* Especially because I'd worked in property for over fifteen years and it's a very profitable industry to be in. But I had to be brave and make the change to start truly living on purpose.

As I write this book, I'm still in the start-up phase of my coaching business. I have created and adjusted along the way, experimenting with different offerings, some that have worked and others that haven't. I've had the space to learn and grow, while also seeing the shadow side and experiencing the limiting beliefs. When you decide to do something that is purposeful and meaningful, fear and resistance will inevitably raise their heads to pull you away. The key is to keep on going and to persist with what you've chosen. I know that this business is exactly what I'm meant to be doing, because coaching clients and talking about abundance brings me so much joy. It's fun and I don't see myself as working; I'm just doing what I love.

You might be thinking, *That's all well and good for Jason, but I can't afford to just give up my job and I don't have enough money to start my own business*. I would say don't give up your job but do start allowing yourself space to imagine what you would really love to do. The more you do that, the more you will start moving towards it. When you cultivate good feelings and thoughts, you can cultivate ideas, and opportunities will present themselves. If you're in the depths of hating your job, feeling and experiencing this negativity and lack, then guess what? Lack and dissatisfaction will continue to occur. Start asking yourself, 'What aspects of my work do I actually enjoy now?' Focus on those and give yourself space to grow the positive vibes.

Let me share how this played out for one of my clients Kat. She was a successful lawyer in a large law firm.

She then progressed her career into funds management with Perpetual in various senior legal roles. She had the career status, she was earning amazing money and had the lifestyle to match. But something wasn't right. She realised that she wasn't enamoured by what signalled success in the corporate environment, and she knew she had to leave. She knew she needed to move into something more purposeful that aligned with her values.

She started allowing herself to tune into what she would love to do. She was talented, intelligent and a natural leader. She wanted to be involved in giving back, in doing something that made a difference in the world. She wanted a career congruent with her values, so she gave herself space to explore that. Yes, it was terrifying to make such a big change, but she allowed herself to accept and feel the terror, knowing that it would right itself when ready.

From that place she was presented with the opportunity to join Grameen Australia as their CEO. Grameen activates social business in Australia and Asia by providing micro loans. It is a perfect fit for Kat's experience and talents, but also fulfils her desires and sense of purpose.

If you do what is purposeful and joyful and you're doing what you love, you don't work a day in your life. It's our divine right to live our lives with purpose and joy. And why not?

Reflection time:

- ⇒ What did you love as a child and as a teenager?
- ⇒ When you review your career to date, what themes are consistent?
- ⇒ What are you naturally good at?
- ⇒ What interests and moves you?

⇒ What do you spend most of your time doing?

⇒ What lights you up?

What if I don't know what my purpose is?

You need to be absolutely okay with the fact that you might not know what your purpose is yet. The more you have an intention to let it unfold and are okay with not knowing immediately what your purpose is, the more it will show itself to you. Remember, we evolve and change as time goes on and so may your purpose. Give yourself the space to be curious about what is purposeful to you and whatever gives you joy. Keep reaching for that. Joy is the indicator that you're on track.

Chapter Nine

Are We Really Spiritual Beings?

I've talked about how we can't always see the big picture for ourselves, but when we intuitively move towards what gives us joy and is purposeful it will unfold. I know for myself that the more I have created this focus and continue to move towards it, the more that has been awakened in me.

I'm going to answer the question that is posed in this chapter title by sharing some personal experiences with you. I'll also share some scientific resources that will help you understand these beliefs.

As you read this chapter, I encourage you to be curious about what might open up for you. Be inquisitive about how powerful you actually are and what is truly available to you.

When I started out on my personal growth journey over 15 years ago, I was very much interested in what I could create in the tangible world – material things, money and better relationships.

While I believed that there was something far greater than my physical self and my personal needs and wants, and I understood that we could manifest when we're aligned energetically, I didn't go very deep with the spiritual side of things. I was given umpteen books about these subjects but couldn't manage to read them. There was talk of how we are all connected (in fact, that we are all one) and I learnt that when we go deep into presence, we could go into states of bliss.

For many years, I just couldn't comprehend that. I wouldn't allow myself to go deep into long meditations, preferring to stick with shorter guided meditations, because my ego made me believe that I only needed to do short meditations. Somehow, I believed that anything longer was taking time away from actually making things happen. This of course was untrue.

During this time, I certainly experienced the benefits of ThetaHealing, kinesiology, Emotional Freedom Technique, reiki and energy healings, every time feeling different and energised (even completely healing psoriasis that I'd experienced from my early thirties), I now know I just wasn't ready for a deeper experience at that time.

We get what we're ready to learn

Hindsight has taught me that we will learn when we're *ready* to learn; sometimes that learning comes from a significant event or experience and at other times it's much subtler.

2014 was a huge year for me. In the January I married Garrett and it was a beautiful, perfect wedding. We had all our loved ones there and our mothers walked us down the aisle. It was such a special moment for me. My mum had always been accepting of me and always allowed me to find my own way in my life without judging my choices. She taught me to be independent and always encouraged me. I had such deep love and appreciation for her as I walked with her towards Garrett, and it took all my strength to keep the tears at bay. The emotion I felt towards her was overwhelming, as was the enormous gratitude I felt at being able to marry my love – something that when I came out as a gay man, I never thought would be possible.

In March of that year Mum announced that she was selling up in Auckland and retiring back to Napier where her twin sister had returned to and where we grew up. I volunteered to help her house hunt and we had a great time. In fact, we found the perfect house for her.

On the five-hour drive back to Auckland she said to me that she'd been experiencing double vision out of her left eye. I told her she'd better get it looked at. Mum had suffered breast cancer previously and had had a full mastectomy. She had been in remission, however, as it turned out, the breast cancer had metastasised as a tumour behind her eye. Initially she was told it would be treatable with radiotherapy and she began her treatment just as she was moving to Napier. However, by August she was not able to hold her food down, so much so that she had to be hospitalised. After much testing it turned out that she had malignant tumours all through her digestive system, meaning that she couldn't process food and that the cancer was terminal.

I decided then and there that I was going to stay with her as often as I could through this time, and ideally keep her at home as much as possible. It was the toughest experience of my life, not only dealing with the terminal prognosis but also the fallout and reactions in my family which were challenging but also understandable.

I started reading Neale Donald Walsch's book, *Home with God,* a book about death and dying. This book gave me great comfort knowing that Mum wasn't really dying but rather that she was just moving into another realm. It talked about what happens when you pass over and also the process of dying. It was very powerful for me. I read this poem to Mum, *The Prayer for the Dying,* and for me it summarises the teachings of the entire book:

> *The God of your understanding is with you now, even in this hour, at this precise moment. If you have no understanding of God, that will not matter. God is still here, in this place with you right now, whispering to your soul, 'You are welcome, whenever you are ready to come home.'*
>
> *You shall not be turned away, not for any cause or reason. If there be cause or reason you believe to be valid, God – should you want God to – invalidates it. God – should*

you want God to – in this moment erases it. God – should you want God to – in this moment makes all paths clear, all roads straight, saying, 'Make way for my beloved, who chooses to be Home with God.'

This prayer is offered for you, wonderful child of the universe, as you embark on the most joyful journey you have ever taken, filled with wondrous surprises. A journey into the greatest happiness you have ever known, and the grandest experience you will ever have.

Dream now of glorious things. Dream of every fantasy come true. Dream of every pain disappearing, of everything of which time has robbed you being given back to you again. Dream of seeing loved ones once more – those who have gone before and those who will follow.

Know for a certainty that when you leave here, you will be again with all those who have held a place in your heart and have gone before. And do not worry about those you leave behind, for you will see them, too, again and again, and love them too again and again, through all eternity, and even in the present moment. For there can be no separation where there is love, and no waiting where there is only Now.

Smile, then, at the joyful anticipation of what is in store. These gifts have been laid up for you, and God has only been waiting for you to return Home to receive them. Peace, joy, and love are you, and are yours, now and always. So it is, and so it shall be, forever and ever. Amen.

When Mum fell unconscious, she was admitted to the hospice and I stayed with her through the week up until she passed away. It was a very hard time but a very powerful time. During that period, I made her a promise. I said to her that while she was going, I was here staying, so I would make the best of my life and create some sort of legacy. I made her that promise.

At the hospice I had my own separate room for family, which was down the hall from Mum. Two nights before she passed away, I awoke at 1 am, finding it hard to breathe. Somehow in that moment I realised it was Mum who was struggling, and I ran down to her room. I could tell she was in distress and I was able to call the nurse who administered her some pain management medication.

While I wanted to be there when Mum passed away on the Sunday morning, I decided that I would give her some space in case she wanted to go in her own way. I needed to do some laundry anyway, so I went home to Mum's. It was such a glorious sunny spring day that I decided to go for a walk up to my favourite spot in Napier, the botanical gardens. As I was walking, I got this feeling in my heart, almost like a jolt, that Mum had just gone. I had my NZ phone on me so I thought I would be getting a call any minute, but when I got home, I found the hospice had been calling me on my Australian mobile; sure enough, Mum had passed.

Once I got back to Sydney after Mum's passing, I decided to go and see Rosemary Butterworth. I'd been seeing Rosemary for some years for healing and guidance. Rosemary is an energy healer, clairvoyant and clairaudient. I thought it was a good idea to have an energy healing after the traumatic period of losing Mum.

When I arrived at Rosemary's she said, 'I'm so glad you're here, I need to tell you that I've started channelling and an Ascended Master wants to come through with a message for you.' She asked me, 'Are you okay with that?' Intrigued, I said yes. So, Rosemary tuned in, dropped out and all of a sudden, a big deep booming voice came out of her saying, 'Hello, my name is Master Korton. I am here to tell you that you are here to help others with abundance. You are already doing this whether you know it or not.' He then shared a couple of conversations that I'd had with others, which really opened them up. He then went on to say, 'If you commit to this, we will support you all along the way.' He continued, 'Do not commit to us yet as it is coming up to your festive season, but if you commit, we will be here for you.'

I recorded it and listened to the message a few times and I was intrigued.

That New Year's Eve, after many champagnes on my balcony, I said, 'Okay, I commit. I commit to being supported and I commit to helping others with abundance.'

Experiences to support the choice

And that's exactly what has happened. In January of 2015, I was asked to join a mastermind group called the Soul Alignment Program which was facilitated by a coach and some of my friends were already part of. While it was a significant financial investment, it was an immediate 'yes' to the work. We were to align ourselves to our soul's purpose.

I shared what I knew about abundance. It started by gathering a few friends together over breakfast. It then expanded into larger Abundance Breakfasts, and then that progressed into one-to-one coaching. Throughout the year we went on a number of retreats. The first one was in Bali. The week before we departed, Garrett and I hosted a party. It was a very boozy affair and we all went out on the town afterwards, much of which I don't remember. The thing I do remember is waking up in the entrance foyer of my apartment.

So, when I arrived in Bali, I was still feeling the effects of that big night and as we arrived on retreat it was announced that we were going into five days of silence with a journal and breakout sessions. Needless to say, my drinking came up and I got very clear with myself that I had been a binge drinker my whole adult life and that it was no longer working for me. I also clarified why I binge drank, which for me was all about socialising.

One of the main reasons was that I didn't like being around drunk people because of the experiences I'd had as a boy with my father. Strangely, instead of not drinking at all, I got drunk to feel comfortable around other drunk people. I also used alcohol to fit in and to escape. It became clear that if I was to be my higher self it meant that I needed to give up alcohol. I knew that it was a massive decision but that if I committed to it, I had to see it through. And I did. I gave up alcohol completely for two years. What resulted was an opening of my connection to the universe. My intuition became sharper, my connection to source became stronger and of course my health and vitality improved.

One of my early clients is a lady by the name of Julia who is a beautiful person and a very spiritually-connected being who is a sound and energy healer as well as an earth worker. I was supporting her in grounding her business to help her make it a financial success. The wonderful gift from working with her was that we called in the angels, the guides, the Ascended Masters and the beings of love and light. It was a space that showed me how connected we are to other beings in the non-physical realm. During that period, I regularly visited Rosemary and she told me that there is an Ascended Master Kuthumi with me. She said that I could call on him to be with me in service to any clients I was working with. Of course, I called him in when I was working with Julia.

One busy real-estate day (I was juggling coaching and my real estate business for a while) I had an online session booked in with Julia. The office was full of people, so I knew I had to conduct her session from the car. I drove around the corner into the middle of Surry Hills, Sydney, and dialled her in; I also called in the full support of the non-physical team including Master Kuthumi. As I was coaching her, I had this feeling come over me that there was another energy present. It was like intuition, only stronger. I said to Julia, 'I think there is a message that wants to come through for you; are you okay if I try to bring it through?' She was an enthusiastic yes. I became highly present and allowed my rational mind to quiet. The next thing I knew, there was another voice coming through me with a specific message for Julia. That was my first experience of channelling.

A week after that first experience of channelling I headed to Kenya on another retreat. I'd told my dear friend, teacher and now colleague, Gisele, about the channelling. As we arrived into our first session with the fourteen other attendees Gisele announced to us, 'Now Master Khutumi is going to come through.' Talk about being thrown in the deep end! But as I allowed myself to be present the channelling came through, and from then on during that retreat I was channelling messages for each of the attendees that were powerful and, in some instances, healing and activating. I also interviewed Master Khutumi on camera and asked my own questions, which was an incredible experience for me. It was during this trip that I clarified with myself that I didn't have to abstain from alcohol any longer. To this day though, I drink very minimally.

Directly after my trip to Africa I headed to Toronto for a week-long conference run by Bob Proctor, the grandfather of the Law of Attraction work. This was a huge event with over 200 attendees. Each morning I was receiving guided messages of, 'Are you going to tell them about the channelling?' But I resisted each day.

The day before the final day, we had the opportunity to go around each table and pitch for two minutes. I realised that it was now or never, and while I didn't channel right then in front of them, I did talk about what was happening through me. This was powerful because it opened up connection with the other attendees. I had people coming up to me asking about it and I would inevitably channel a message to them. At the eleventh hour I stepped into my truth, my authenticity and made some wonderful connections and new friends.

As I returned to Sydney, I knew that the channelling would form part of my work as a coach.

Up until that period I called myself the Abundance Advocate, but I realised now I was actually activating abundance in those I worked with. And so, the Abundance Activator brand was launched.

My next big experience was on another visit to Rosemary. She told me that the Galactic Beings of Love were with her and that they were here to take me on a journey. I lay on her healing table and we became very present, and all of a sudden, I went into a deep meditation. At first, I was experiencing bright lights and then I could feel myself going on a journey somewhere, almost as if I was on a flying carpet. It was familiar and I felt safe and comfortable. The next thing I experienced was an overwhelming feeling of love moving through me. I could feel and sense how we are all connected by this frequency of love. It was powerful and divinely beautiful.

As I came back to the room, I felt like I was on a drug induced high. I was in love with everything! I had to hug Rosemary and her husband John. Everything looked absolutely wondrous to me, even the most mundane things.

The plants particularly looked vibrantly alive. It was quite incredible and something that will always stay with me. What it showed me is how we *are* love and how we are all connected by the energy of love. This euphoric feeling stayed with me for a long time.

My next powerful experience was after attending a talk by the acclaimed author of *The Power of Now* and *A New Earth*, Eckhart Tolle, who was speaking at the Sydney Convention and Exhibition Centre. Strangely, I have no memory of what he talked about, but his presence on stage was incredible. It was his presence that activated a deep level of presence in myself. As I left the centre, I felt very connected and present. The next morning, I went into very deep meditation and decided to go and walk around Sydney Park. It was a beautiful, sunny and still morning, and I realised that I was noticing everything in a very expansive way.

I continued to take everything in; the trees, the plants, the sun, the air, the people and the dogs. Everything was beautiful. As I walked further into the park, I sensed a deep state of bliss moving through me. This experience showed me how powerful we are when we allow ourselves to see what is right there in the very present moment.

The next big experience was during the first two-day retreat that I co-facilitated with Gisele. We had arranged for Tammy, a wonderful healer, to be at this retreat to conduct healings and to bring her beautiful energy to the space. Because Tammy works very much intuitively, we asked her to conduct healings as and when she felt. Day two arrived and she hadn't conducted any healings. When we asked her what was happening, she said, 'Well, actually, I'm only being guided that I am to conduct a healing on you, Jason.' I was initially surprised as I thought I was there as the facilitator and that I wasn't there to be healed. I received a clear message that if this was so, it needed to happen in front of everyone.

So, we got the healing table out into the middle of the room and Tammy became present and began to bring through her healing energy for me. As she did, I felt like I was levitating. My whole body spasmed and I was crying uncontrollably. It was an incredibly emotional experience, but also very powerful for the attendees to witness.

I'd already booked in to see Rosemary for an energy healing the day after the retreat, as I thought it would be a good thing to do for myself after two days of facilitating. Again, she said that the Galactic Beings of Love were there and that they wanted to support me in my growth, and another powerful activation happened to my physical body – I was spasming and crying and I felt like something enormous had changed in my being.

The next day I was at my Sydney apartment meditating and I could feel that there was some sound that wanted to come through me. As I allowed it, this very digital, very fast sound came out of me. I realised that it was light language, which is a multidimensional language with dynamic frequency encodings of sound and light and is understood on a soul level. It was coming through really fast and I felt as if my whole system had sped up, as if I was hyperactive. I'd experienced receiving light language before, but I'd never channelled it myself. Fortunately, I knew that my friend Michael Muir, who is also a healer, had been channelling light language for many years. I phoned him to ask what was happening to me and he explained that my body was simply adjusting to the frequency that was moving through me. He channelled similar sound to me and slowed it down so that my body could adjust to the frequency and power of it.

Ever since then I've had the gift of channelled light language. I often use it in leading my clients into meditation. Sometimes it's digital sounding, sometimes it's earthy, sometimes I sing and sometimes a high-pitched frequency comes through. I step out of the way and allow the light language to come through me. It's easy for me to access this language, as it can't be deciphered by the rational mind, unlike the channelled messages. My clients get what they need from it: sometimes there are healings, activations and bodily responses and other times the response is subtle. But I try not to label or judge it, or even have any expectations from it.

This past year I attended Vipassana, a ten-day silent meditation retreat. It was incredibly powerful. It deepened my meditation practice by encouraging me to sit on the floor for long periods and meditate, allowing my mind to slow down and my body to experience the energy and stillness at a much more profound level.

All of these experiences have left a lasting impression on me. At times, I've been able to get myself back into similar states of bliss as the experience I had in Sydney Park. In meditation I've also been able to experience powerful responses to my energy centres; seeing bright lights and colours running through me with my chakras (my energy centres) opening.

These experiences have all arrived unexpectedly. At times they were unexplainable, but they have all come at the right time and only when I was ready. I don't know if I'll have any other similar experiences, but I'm as open as I've ever been, and I believe it's that openness that allows us that connection into our power and spirituality. I know that for the clients that I work with, when they are open to receiving, they do in fact receive, and their experience is deeper.

To read further about this area of study, Dr Joe Dispenza and Dr Bruce Lipton have been collating the science behind how humans are both multi-dimensional and more than just physical beings. You might also like to look up Abraham Hicks. Esther Hicks channels Abraham, and their work is all about the teachings of the Law of Attraction. They've created powerful meditations called 'Getting into the Vortex' that you might like to experience.

While I've had – and continue to have – activations that can't be understood by the rational mind, and as I bring forth what's in front of me to use in service to everyone that I work with, it's proven to me time and again just how powerful we are. Yet I feel that I've only just touched the surface. I feel that there is so much more we can open up to. As I continue to surrender and allow myself to be this spiritual being, I know that I'm able to give more to those who are in my life, and in whatever way is right for them.

I say to you, dear reader, the more you move forward with an openness and a curiosity to the magnificence your life has to offer, the more you practice the tools I've shared with you in this book and the more abundance you will experience in your life.

We all came here to live abundantly and to experience heaven on Earth. Let's do it together.

Testimonials

'I've loved working with Jason. He is kind, caring and insightful! He helped me focus on creating a better me and releasing all that's negative. I will miss our sessions.'

Candys Navon, Melbourne, July 2019

'Wow! Working with Jason has given me clarity and focus. He is an absolutely gifted and beautiful human being. I have complete trust in his ability to lead me into my own truth. Thanks, Jason. You've really helped me!'

Monique Low, New Zealand, July 2019

'Dear Jason, I loved working with you in your capacity as an Abundance Activator. Through your process I was able to get out of my head and into a place of truth where clear downloads were available to me. I could see clearly what was truly important to me, what my Land of Abundance looked like, what steps were needed to achieve my most desired outcomes and how to operate from a place of my own personal power.

Because of this I was able to resolve a particularly difficult investment situation and had a very large sum of money paid to me with ease and grace when it previously looked certain that I would have to go to court and fight and with a possibility of losing it all and more. I would highly recommend you and would love to work with you again in the future.'

Sasha Balding, Sydney, July 2019

'Working with Jason is pure joy, his ability to cut through the bullshit and unleash the gold is inspiring and impressive. The grounded inspired actions that come from working with Jason is where the value lies in his work. He definitely keeps you on your toes while gently grounding you in inspired actions that allow the activation of abundance to come to the surface'

Di Foster, Christchurch, August 2018

'I have no idea if what Jason does is spiritual or not, but what I do know is that it works. Focusing your mind on what you want and understanding what you need to do to get there is incredibly powerful and most definitely yields results.
My very strong advice would be to take some time to work with Jason, it will be more than worth your while.'

Richard Hardy, Sydney, September 2017

'How do I begin to explain the positive change that's come into my life since working with Jason? We've been working together for roughly two years, and my perspective, my abundance and my spiritual connection has transformed incredibly. He is more than a coach, he is a confidant and above all a great friend. His ability to bring forth your purpose and abundance in life is second to none. Since working with Jason, not only has my spiritual abundance transformed but my financial abundance has changed beyond belief. I've kicked so many life goals within the two years that I never thought would be possible before. I can't thank you enough Jason! I have no hesitations in recommending him to anyone and everyone.'

Joanna Younan, Sydney, May 2019

About the Author

Jason Snaddon is the Abundance Activator. Jason helps his clients vibrationally align to abundance in all areas of their life – business, finances, health, wellbeing and relationships.

Jason started studying the principles he teaches in 2005 when he was struggling to feel successful within the property industry. He wasn't happy being the poorest performer in his company. He learned that your focus creates your reality. He clarified what he wanted in his life and on what his Land of Abundance was. Within five years, by consistently doing the work, keeping a clear focus, vibrationally aligning to his vision and following his inspired actions along the way, his Land of Abundance unfolded. He built his own successful real estate business, Love Property, bought his penthouse apartment, found a beautiful loving relationship and achieved financial freedom by the time he was 45.

After losing his mum to cancer in 2014, he began exploring his greater purpose and his truth at a deeper level. What has unfolded is a uniquely powerful ability to channel and activate the abundance that is currently within all of us. In this book he pulls together what he practises in his life and teaches and activates within his clients as the Abundance Activator.

Reference List

Chapter Two

Graham, L. Linda Graham MFT, 'The Triangle of Victim, Rescuer, Persecutor'. Available online at: lindagraham-mft.net. Accessed on 15th July 2019.

Chapter Seven

Bernstein, G (2018) Judgement Detox Journal: A Guided Exploration, California, Hay House.

Hicks, E & J (2006) The Law of Attraction: The Basic Teachings of Abraham, California, Hay House.

Activate and Manifest a Life beyond your wildest dreams

Notes

www.ingramcontent.com/pod-product-compliance
Lightning Source LLC
Chambersburg PA
CBHW071628080526
44588CB00010B/1324